DRAWING
AND DESIGN
for
Embroidery

For "The Goblins" with love.

DRAWING AND DESIGN

for Embroidery

A course for the fearful

Richard Box

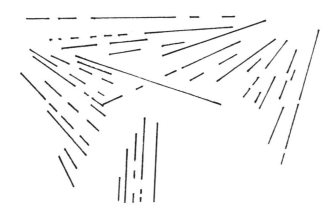

B.T. Batsford Ltd, London

© Richard Box 1988
First published 1988
Reprinted 1989, 1992

This paperback edition first published 1995

ISBN 0 7134 7883-7

Typeset by Servis Filmsetting Ltd., Manchester
Printed and bound in Great Britain by
The Bath Press, Avon
for the publishers
B.T. Batsford Ltd.
4 Fitzhardinge Street
London W1H 0AH

CONTENTS

ACKNOWLEDGEMENTS

I am indebted to many organizations and individuals for their part in the production of this book. I now take this happy opportunity to give them my thanks for all their encouragement and help.

To the Embroiderers' Guild, the National Gallery and the Victoria & Albert Museum for permission to use examples of work from their collections.

To Jan Beaney, Hilary Bower, Miranda Brookes, Sally Burwell, Barbara Buttle, Julia Caprara, Robin Giddings, Jo Gregory, Gill Hervey-Murray, Joan Hoare, Heide Jenkins, Jean Littlejohn, Jean Mooney, Michael Moore, Jennie Parry, Eirian Short, Mariel Stapleton, Verina Warren and Lily Westerop for their valuable contributions.

To Rachel Wright, my editor, for her useful guidance and kind assurances.

Especially to Jo Pickering for her time and patience in typing the manuscript and retyping the seemingly endless amendments and alterations.

Finally, to all those students who have enjoyed my courses. To all of you who have been my mentors and without whose presence this book would not have been possible.

Story time – The Giant

Once upon a time in a nearby valley there lived some people. Now, these people never dared to move from their valley because whenever they tried to do so by climbing the surrounding hills, they were met by an enormous giant who roared at them most ferociously. They were so terrified that they ran back into their valley as fast as ever their legs would carry them . . . determined never to venture forth again.

This had been going on for hundreds of years until, one day, a new and brave king was chosen from among them. And he thought to himself, 'This simply isn't good enough! We never meet new people, never develop our trade and never make new friends. Indeed, we are becoming very dull, ignorant and boring.' The new king decided to journey out of the valley and beyond the hills all by himself and in spite of all dangers. He set off out of the valley with some feelings of trepidation and expected the giant to appear at any moment. Sure enough the giant appeared, horribly enormous and roaring most ferociously. However, instead of running away as all of his people had done before, the king took one step forward. To his amazement the giant became one inch shorter. Thus encouraged, the king took another step forward and the giant became another inch shorter. Eventually, when the king came right up to the giant he was so small that the king could hold him in his hand. The king then asked the giant his name. The giant replied, 'My name is fear.'

INTRODUCTION

Dear Reader,

For many years members of the Embroiderers' Guild who have attended my courses have asked me, 'When are you going to write a book?' and for many years my reply was, 'I couldn't possibly, I change my mind too often and I disagree today with what I said yesterday!' However, over the past five years I have been asked repeatedly to run two of my courses again and again. These are the two which are planned for beginners, and I call them, 'Design for the Nervous and Anxious' and 'Drawing for the Terrified and Afraid'. I have, as a result, begun to realize that, although I adapt and develop these courses each time I teach them, there are certain elements and aspects that do not change. Consequently, I have taken the plunge and decided to commit myself to paper.

Are you an accomplished and expert embroiderer, who also feels 'stuck' in an approach to designing, drawing and embroidery techniques and would like to start at the beginning again? If so, this book is especially for you. Are you an absolute beginner who does not know how to design and draw for embroidery and, moreover, are you terrified of starting? If so, this book is even more especially for you. There are probably many reasons for your fearfulness, but whatever they are, one tiny little spark is remaining: you still *want* to be able to draw and make your own designs. This must be so, otherwise you would not be reading this book, which is devised to help you step by step. Now, read the story opposite about the giant before going any further.

This story was told to me not so long ago when I was very worried about something that was about to happen. It helped me enormously to face this 'something' and also helped me to realize that I was worried by my own imagining and not actuality. The 'giant' was in my head! Needless to say, when this 'something' eventually happened it was nothing like I had imagined it would be. My worries were unjustified. You too, just by reading this far, have taken your first step in overcoming your fear.

I now need to urge you to read each chapter of this book in turn and to do each of the exercises one after the other. Treat this book as a *progressive course*. I call the exercises games because they are fun to do. Each game leads onto the next and all subsequent games contain the underlying principles of the preceding ones. If you play all the games in succession you will overcome your fear and gain confidence in your abilities with ease.

You are now embarking upon a wonderful voyage of discovery.

Fig. 1 — *The value of simplicity.*

Two Figures in the Rain. *Embroidery, Miss E. Griffiths, 1930. (Collection of the Embroiderers' Guild)*

Not only is this embroidery very small (6.1cm wide × 7.6cm high) but very poor materials have been applied and enhanced by very ordinary stitching to depict an event that we have all experienced. A rich evocation has been achieved in an extraordinarily simple way.

Simplicity is not an end in art, but one arrives at simplicity in spite of oneself, in approaching the real sense of things. Simplicity is complexity itself and one has to be nourished by its essence in order to understand its value.
                                    Constantin Brancusi

The medium is as unimportant as myself, only the forming counts.
                                    Kurt Schwitters

Less is more.
                                    Ludwig Mies Van De Rohe

Chapter One

PREPARATION

As with many other activities the way to enjoy making your own designs and drawings resides in the actual *process* of creating them rather than in the end products alone. Swami Vivekananda wrote, 'Proper attention to the finishing, strengthening of the means is what we need. With the means all right the end must come.' This has the same emphasis as the adage, 'To travel hopefully is better than to arrive.' The analogy of a journey is very helpful. We all need to prepare ourselves for a journey, so try this first exercise.

Exercise 1 – Letting go

First of all, sit in an upright chair and completely relax. Go all floppy! Allow your spine to rest against the back of your chair and let your arms dangle down by your sides like soggy spaghetti. Remain like this for a minute or two, and in doing so let go of all your worries,

Fig. 2 — Snow Scene. *Charcoal drawing, Richard Box, 1982.*

problems and anxieties. Actually say to each one of them in turn, 'just go over there will you? I don't need you now, if at all, and certainly not for the next two minutes.' As you do this, also become aware of the tensions in the various parts of your body gradually becoming more relaxed as you allow yourself to become more rested and at ease.

Henceforth this will be known as the *soggy spaghetti arm exercise*. When we go on a journey we need to take only that luggage which is necessary. We need to dispense with unnecessary burdens. So practise this exercise often and particularly whenever you feel tense and anxious. You could do it just before you go to bed at night in order to help you sleep.

The next exercise also helps you relax but at the same time its intention is to wake you up and make you alert.

Exercise 2 – The golden cord

Rousseau once said, 'Everything that comes to the mind enters through the gate of sense.' The senses of sight, hearing, touch, taste and smell operate for most of us very well. Some of us have one or two which are impaired or do not function at all. If this is so, then it is necessary to enjoy those that do function perfectly or impaired. We tend to take the operation of our senses very much for granted. Just imagine what life for us would be like if none of them worked! So, try this exercise for making you relaxed and attentive. Remain sitting in your upright chair. Allow both feet to rest gently on the ground. Avoid unnecessary tension like pressing your feet hard on the ground as if you were trying to push

the floor boards six feet further down! Space your feet slightly apart. Keep your bottom well back upon the seat of your chair but do not now let your spine touch the back of the chair; allow it to be self-supporting. A useful way to achieve this is to imagine a glittering golden cord attached to the top of your head that is suspended from heaven. The piano teacher who taught me this analogy said that the golden cord is not rigid or tense but hung just securely enough to allow the body to be relaxed and alert simultaneously.

Now allow your mind to attend first to the sense of touch working. To begin with, notice the gentle pressure of your bottom on the seat of your chair and then your feet on the ground. Indeed, notice the touch of your feet inside your socks, stockings or tights. Notice the touch of all your clothes around the various parts of your body such as your calves, knees, thighs, stomach, shoulders and arms. Notice the touch of the cuffs on your wrists and the collar on your neck. Notice also how you can feel the play of air around your hands and wrists, your neck and face. Notice the touch of the air as you breathe in through your nostrils and out through your mouth.

Then allow your mind to be attentive to the sense of hearing. Start first with the sounds of your own body. Begin with the sound of your breathing. Allow your breath to flow as before. Do not force any deliberate breathing movements. Let it be easy. Listen to the differences in sounds of your inward taking and outward letting of breath. Listen also to that tiny space of silence in between each inward and outward breath. Now let your listening move to the sounds in the room. These may be the ticking of a clock or an occasional squeak in your chair. Then, let your listening move beyond the room to the sounds in the house and extend to those outside the building. These may be bird song, traffic and even your neighbours quarrelling! Whatever the sounds are, allow them to come to your hearing and listen to them without your mind becoming too annoyed with one or over delighted with another. If you do, you may become attached to it and want to hold on to it even when it has gone. This will prevent you from hearing the next sound because you will be 'listening' to your imagination instead. Therefore, as each sound goes, let it go, and without criticism accept and be attentive to each and every sound as it arises. *Be particularly attentive to the sound of silence.* It is significant that many have believed in the importance of silence. The Desiderata begins, 'Go placidly amid the noise and haste and remember what peace there may be in silence.' Mozart, when asked what he considered to be the most important element in his music replied, 'The silence'.

Next, and lastly, allow your eyes to open very slowly. Try to avoid opening them wide too quickly because the glare of light might be painful. Now become aware of an object which your eyes immediately fall upon. According to Leonardo da Vinci the eye is 'the window of the soul'. Try to avoid casting your eyes around looking for something 'interesting'; simply look at the first thing you see. If you *give* your interest to something, you will find it interesting. So, start by looking at the shape of the object. Look at its *outer edges* and its *inner contours*. Notice the variations of curved and straight lines which compose the whole shape. Now look at the *tonal values* of this object. Notice the variations between the very light and very dark tones. Now look at the *colours* of this object. However many or however few, notice the variety of the colours and their hues. Then, note the setting of this object and its context. Look above it, look below it, look to its right and to its

left. Notice, in such places, the same kind of variety of edges and boundaries, of tones and of colours. Finally, become aware of the connection and interrelationship between all things; as Alexander Pope once said, 'All are but parts of one stupendous whole.'

So much, and it is much, for this exercise. It will be known henceforth as the *golden cord exercise*. It is an important one because without it the following exercises will not work to advantage. John Ruskin once said 'I would rather teach drawing that my pupils may learn to love nature than to teach the looking at nature that they may learn to draw.' The meaning of this statement will become more and more apparent as you proceed through this book. However, already you have noticed, by practising this exercise, how wonderful is the natural operation of your senses and how enjoyable it is to observe each of them working in turn by disciplining your mind to attend in this way. What could be more natural than that?

> *The eye that sees is the I experiencing itself in what it sees. It becomes self-aware, it realizes that it is an integral part of the great continuum of all that is. It sees things such as they are.*
> Frederick Franck

Fig. 3 — Daisies. *Embroidery (detail), Richard Box, 1985.*

You will be interested to know that I first
learned the rudiments of the exercise
from a Benedictine nun. She called it
prayer. It is the first part of a simple form
of meditation. Indeed, it was she who
gave me the revelation that such
activities as drawing, painting, and
embroidery need not be self-indulgent
pastimes but activities of great import, of
devotion, even of prayer.

There is no sin in painting, if that is what your instinct draws you to all the time. Painting and looking especially when you understand what kind of 'subjects' have that deep close affinity to contemplative prayer. They are both means of opening a door, not onto wishful thinking but onto realities not accessible by less reflective and absorbed means. Prayer follows on contact with these realities whether it is contact within a mass of poppies or those white daisies. . . .

Sister Columba O.S.B.

Fig. 4 — Daisies. *Pencil drawing, Richard Box, 1982.*

PREPARATION

Exercise 3 –
The sheet of the senses

Prepare yourself and your equipment in the following manner. First of all practise the soggy spaghetti arm and the golden cord exercises. Next, maintaining the attention of the latter exercise, clip a sheet of A3 cartridge paper to a drawing board and sharpen two pencils, a soft one and a hard one such as 2B and 2H. Then, place your upright chair about three feet away from a table. Rest the board in a comfortable position somewhere between the middle of your thighs and your knees. The edge of the table will act as a support for the upper part of the board to rest on. The format of the board can be either horizontal or vertical and the angle of the board can be anything between 10° and 90°. Indeed, when you practise this exercise try as many variations as possible.

Now, notice that there are four main joints that move in your arm: the knuckles, the wrist, the elbow and the shoulder. Try moving these joints each in turn; then hold one of the pencils near the lead and allow the point to touch the paper. *Without predicting* what kind of marks will occur on the paper, allow marks to occur by simply moving the knuckles. Observe what the resulting marks *look* like. Do this movement again, but this time *listen* to the sound. Do this same movement on the paper again and notice the *touch* of the pencil in your

hand and the kind of vibrations you are feeling as the marks occur. Are you gripping the pencil with terror so that the whites of your knuckles are showing? Or are you becoming more relaxed so that your hold is gentle? In fact, try both a firm and gentle grip. Now hold the pencil further away from the lead, somewhere at the middle. Then allow marks to occur in exactly the same way as before and attend to each of your senses working in the same order. Now hold the pencil at the end furthest away from the lead point and proceed making marks in precisely the same way.

If you are doing this in a relaxed and unselfconscious way you should be discovering that, however slight, the marks look different from each other, and sound and feel different as you make them. So far you have been allowing only your knuckles to move. So now let your wrist move and then your elbow, and finally your shoulder. You have probably used only one hand to hold the pencil, so try the other hand. You have also been using only one pencil, so try the other one. You may have been holding the pencil in only one way such as between your thumb and the first two fingers. Try other ways of holding the pencil and allow the side of the pencil lead as well as its point to make marks on the paper.

If you are still wondering what is supposed to happen, you are probably listening to your questions in your head rather than to the marks occurring on

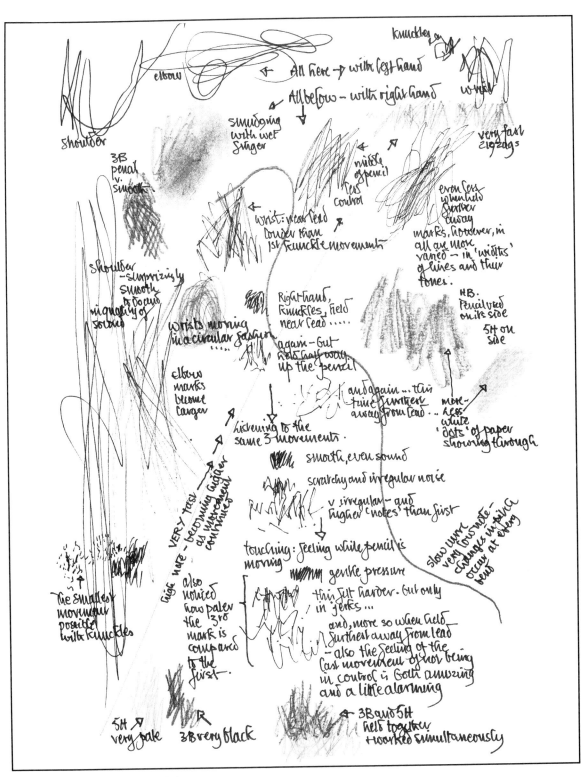

Fig. 5 — *Example of a sheet of the senses.*

the paper. Try again after you have read this analogy. Imagine that you are travelling through uncharted waters on this 'voyage of discovery' of yours. No one has been there before. Certainly you have never been there. You do not know what *will* happen. Therefore, do not expect or predict anything. I promise you that there are no rapids nor crocodiles (unless you conjure them up in your imagination). Instead, there are lovely things to see, hear and touch every time you steer your boat in any direction or at whatever speed. So, all you need to do is to 'steer your boat'. This 'boat' is your arm and hand holding and directing the pencil. You simply have to decide *before* each mark you make where and how to hold the pencil, how fast and how slow you move, in what direction to go and which sense you will attend to. Then make each mark in turn and attend *as* you do it. In this way you will discover wonderful things.

I first used this method of exploring drawing materials with primary school children, who as you can guess, practised it without preconceived ideas, but with ease and enjoyment. You too can discover the nature and properties of the materials you are using: you can find out what they can do and what they like to do. Furthermore you can discover the nature of learning how to learn. Every time you practise this exercise you will learn something new. Soon you will find out that your voyage of discovery never ends and that new delights are waiting to be enjoyed all the time.

You can see from the examples illustrated here that remarks about each mark have been included on these sheets of the senses. After you have practised one or two of your own, try another where you write your own comments too. Try to write each observation immediately *after* you have made each mark.

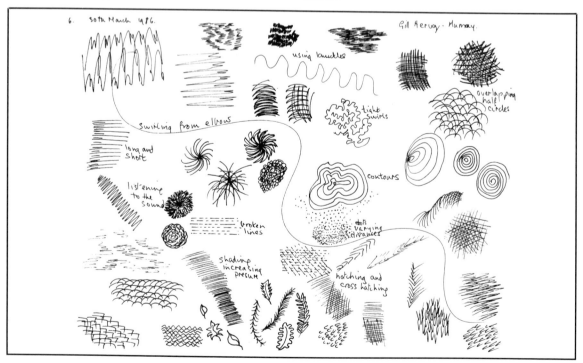

Fig. 6 — *Examples of sheets of the senses.* [Sketches a, b and c, *Gill Hervey-Murray;* d *Sally Burwell;* e (detail) *Michael Moore.*]

6b

PREPARATION

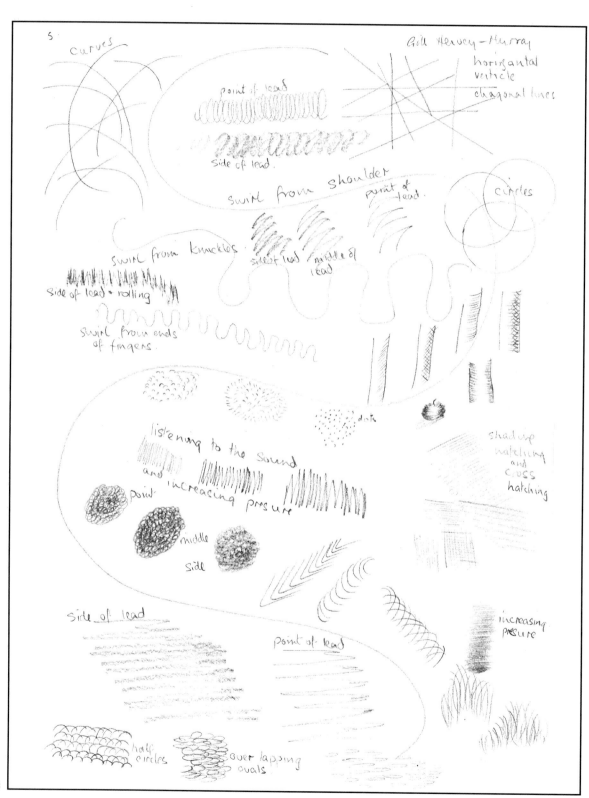

20

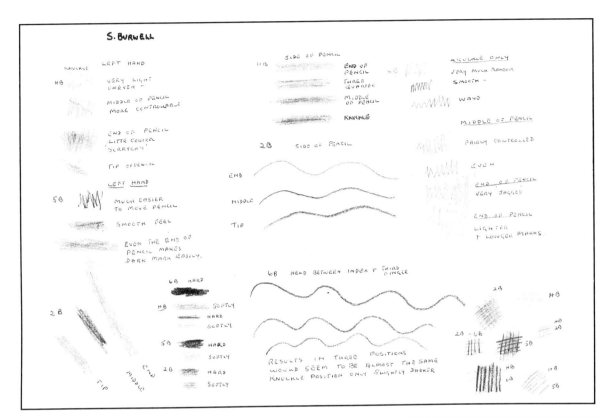

6d

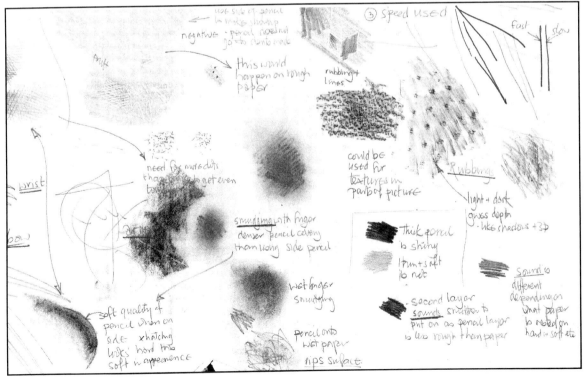

6e

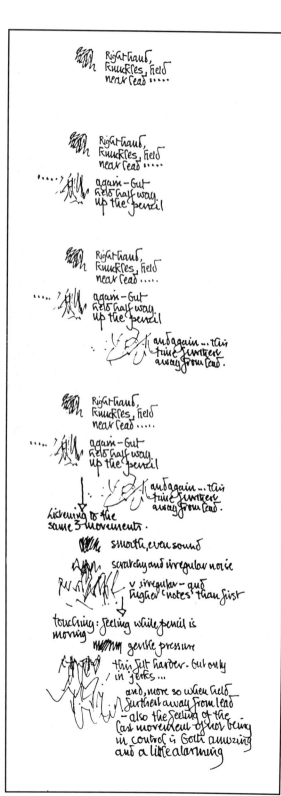

Try to avoid making a lot of marks and then going back trying to remember how you held your pencil or what sound you heard about 30 marks ago. At first you may find the frequent changes from drawing to writing a little awkward. However, with practice you will develop a natural rhythm and find the balance between drawing and writing easy to maintain.

Keep all sheets you make, put them away for a few days and then refer to them from time to time. The purpose of keeping them for reference is to help you remember not only *what* things you have discovered but also *how* you discovered them. Look at the drawing and embroideries illustrated here and notice not so much the representation but rather the quality of marks, their variety and the sensitivity of touch needed by the persons who produced them.

The subsequent exercises will enable you to transfer your newly found forms of knowledge in numerous ways. So try to avoid the temptation of throwing away any manifestation of your knowledge.

Fig. 7 — *The sheet of the senses in process.*

Try to write each of your observations after *you have made each mark.*

Fig. 8 — *The value of the mark and lines as compositional elements.*

Fig. 8a — *Sketch for* Paris Awarding the Golden Apple. *Sepia drawing, Parmigianino (Mazzuola, Francesco Maria), 1503–1540. (Victoria & Albert Museum)*

Francesco Parmigianino has been described as, 'one of the most sensitive and elegant of the early Mannerists'. Observe that within the apparent freedom and looseness of approach there are many subtleties and varieties of marks and lines contained in this drawing.

Fig. 8b — *Pillow cover. Black silk on linen. English (late sixteenth century). (Victoria & Albert Museum)*

Observe within the relative restraint of approach compared with the previous illustration how there are also many subtle and various marks and lines which have been achieved by variations of back, chain, cord, braid and buttonhole stitches.

Fig. 8c — *Detail of a jacket. Gold and silk machine embroidery on 'vanished' muslin. Robin Giddings, 1985.*

Robin Giddings works on the sewing machine with vanishing muslin in new ways to create, as he says, 'A wholly personal textile surface, using the machine to replace the warp and allowing the flowing machine line to combine elements of a precious nature into a web-like structure.'

Observe here and compare with the other illustrations how within an apparent freedom of stitch direction, combined with the firm discipline of just one kind of stitch with only two kinds of thread, a dazzling variety of marks and lines can be achieved.

Chapter Two
THE SERIOUS FUN
IN DESIGNING

Fig. 9 — *The value of the process. Observe how a reflective and absorbed response to one reality leads to another more particular reality.*

Triptych 3. *Embroidery, Miranda Brookes c.1984. Overlays of silk, paper and tissue paper drawn and printed and then embroidered using both hand and machine stitchery.*

'In terms of subject matter, my work over the last few years has developed from a general interest in the landscape garden to a more particular concentration on the tree in its environment. Woodhouse Eaves, where I now live and its surrounding countryside is a stimulating location where the tree emerging from snow, mist, fog, rain and sunshine has become a major source of ideas. A most recent manifestation of this concern is reflected in the mixture of drawn, printed and embroidered imagery in combinations of paper and fabric.'

As with the preceding chapter, this, also, is concerned with the *process*. Its emphasis is upon your learning to enjoy the *doing* and *making* of your *own* designs rather than my giving you a quick recipe for an instant result. In other words, I am concerned with developing you as an individual capable of deciding certain courses of action for yourself and as a unique designer, although you might not believe this yet. Nevertheless, trust me, because I *shall* be giving you certain recipes to follow. As when we first learned to cook we needed some basic recipes to start with. Once we understood some of the main rules, which

are governed by laws and principles, we then modified the recipes and even the rules because we came to understand some of the governing laws and principles. In the same way the recipes, which I give you, will achieve many designs. However, they, and some important rules are here mainly so that you may come to understand some of the laws and principles of designing more easily. In this way you will gain confidence in the production of your work and later on you will be able to transfer these laws and principles to your own invented recipes and rules.

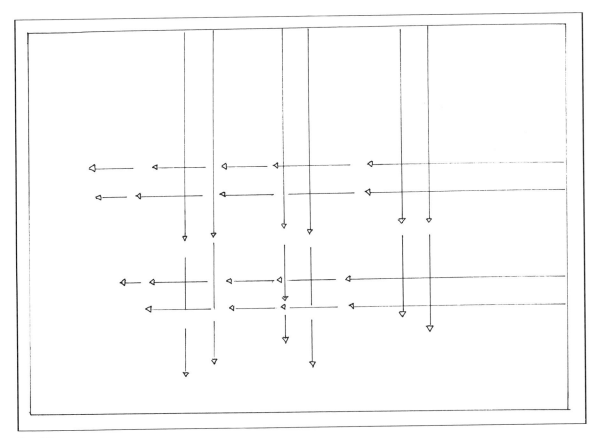

Fig. 10a

Fig. 10b

Exercise 4 –
Composing harmonies with line and shape

Practise the golden cord exercise. If you have lots of time, spend ten minutes doing another sheet of the senses. Both these exercises will help you to become relaxed, alert, and ready for this one.

Clip a sheet of A3-sized cartridge paper onto your drawing board. Place the board in a sloping position so that you remain comfortable as before, and put near you a 2B pencil and a set square. Look at Figs. 10a and b and with the help of your set square draw twelve various sized and proportioned rectangles like those in the illustrations.

Try to keep wide margins between the rectangles and, as you need to maintain as much clarity as possible, erase the cross-over lines within these margins. Within these rectangles you will be making purely abstract compositions of line and shape. Later on you will be using tone and then colour. You will now also be practising a particular design process or way of working which will help you to dispel all your worries and anxieties about the end results. It will help if you liken this design process to a game. Like all enjoyable games, it is fun, but *serious* fun. It is not heavy nor ponderous but light and joyful.

Before you proceed any further, consider the nature of lines. The line has been described as 'the moving point'. It is the initial mark of the drawing instrument on the drawing surface; for example, the pencil point on the paper. Along every line

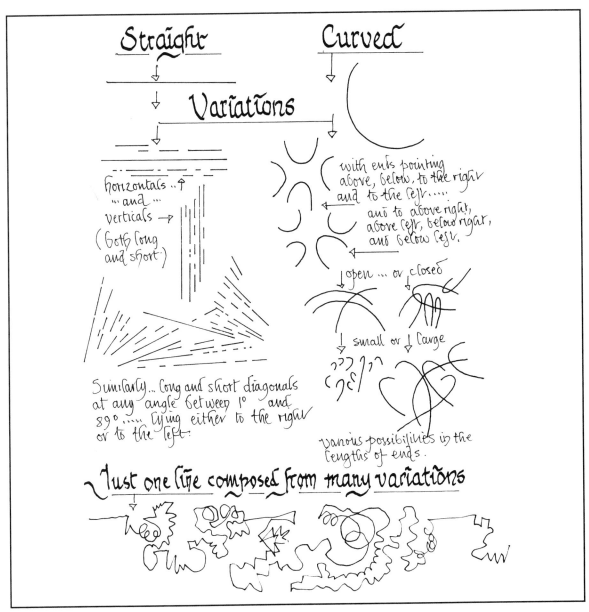

Fig. 10c — Categories of line.

there are thousands of points; indeed, a line is *composed* of points.

Now look at Fig. 10c. There are only two main categories or directions of line. These are the straight and the curved. The straight can vary between vertical, horizontal and diagonal. The curve can be 'open' or 'closed'. Both have many variations between these extremes. I believe that this is all that there is because if you make a very complicated line it is composed of the many variations of straight and curved lines. It will help you to begin to understand that which is simple and straightforward in order to simplify your thinking. This in turn will clarify what you do.

Fig. 10d

Look now at Fig. 10d and once again ensure that you are sitting comfortably by means of the golden cord. Take up your pencil, choose four or five of your twelve rectangles and start drawing some horizontal lines in each of these rectangles. Some can be done with the help of your set square, some freehand. Some can be long and some short, some may touch only the left of the rectangle, some the right. Some can 'float' in the middle and some can go right across. As with the sheet of the senses try to remember to listen to the sounds, to look at what marks occur and to feel the touch of the pencil as it moves across. Moreover, try to remember to hold the pencil in a number of ways in your hand and in a number of positions on the pencil itself. Work with speed. Avoid pausing in your drawing in case you become agitated. Therefore, be restful but alert. This activity should take just about two minutes. Have fun! When you finish take a ten-second 'soggy spaghetti arm' rest, then read on.

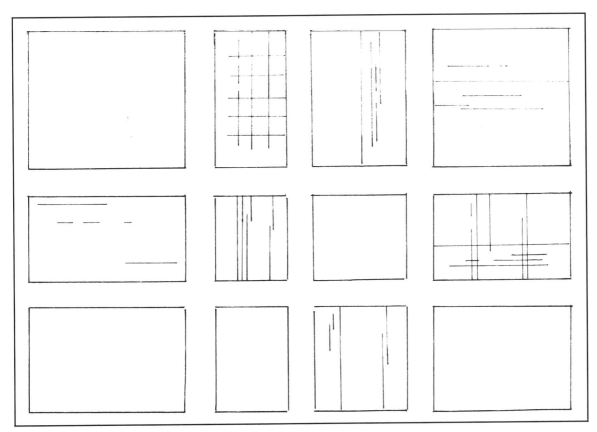

Fig. 10e

Now choose two or three new rectangles and start drawing vertical lines in exactly the same way as you drew your horizontal lines, employing as many variations as possible. In this way also draw some vertical lines where you have already drawn some horizontals, as in Fig. 10e. Then rest for a while.

Now in the same manner draw some diagonals and then some curves and take a short rest between each change of line direction. By the end of five minutes you should have about ten lines in each of your twelve rectangles. You need to have made *some* lines in *all* of your rectangles as in Fig. 10g.

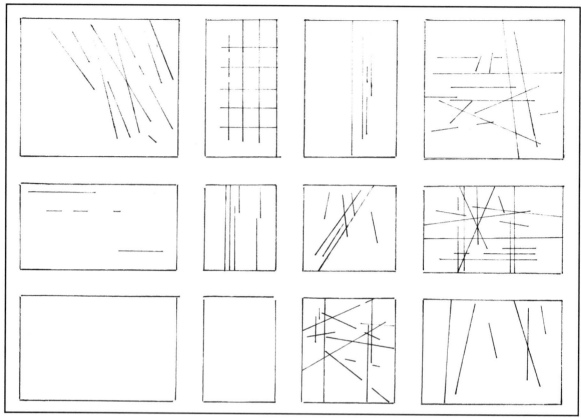

Fig. 10f

Thus far you have played this game of serious fun very well. Do you know that all games have to have rules?

Thus far you have practised all of the seven rules by which this game may be played *already*. However, I need now to explain the rules to you in some detail so that you may use them to your full advantage.

Fig. 10g

> *Rules are part of the game, they are not*
> *outside it. No rules: then no game.*
> *Different rules: then a different game.*
> John Dewey

Rule I – Be restful

You need to be restful in order to direct your passionate energies. This does not mean that you deny or smother such energies. On the contrary, your obedience will help them to grow more fruitfully. To rest also means to remain or to stay. The ability to persevere in work and play is an important asset. So, rests in between activities are important, as indeed is being restful during them. In this way your work and play will flow more easily.

Rule II – Maintain a comfortable posture

The reason for this is allied to the first rule. If you can maintain a comfortable posture that at the same time keeps you alert and concentrates your energies rather than dissipates them you will find ease of mind and heart as well as the body.

Rule III – Attend to the operation of your senses

This rule helps you maintain your concentration and thereby assists your being able to enjoy those delights that are *now* happening. Remember how you enjoyed doing the golden cord exercise and the sheet of the senses.

> *We always live at the time we live and not at some other time, and only by extracting at each present time the full meaning of each present experience are we prepared for doing the same thing in the future.*
>
> John Dewey

> *Human beings typically attend to one sense channel at a time. When we are listening intently to a bird's song, we may not feel a touch, smell a flower, or see a deer. We may not be able to perceive two different auditory messages – one to each ear – coming in at the same time. We choose the one we wish to listen to, and we are temporarily deaf to the other channel. We may think we can attend to many channels of sensory information at once because we shift our attention rapidly and frequently from one event to another. This gives us the impression of continuous perception of many things simultaneously.*
>
> P. Mussen, J. Conger and J. Kagan

Rule IV – Work and play at speed

This really means try not to be distracted by other things while you are actually supposed to be working. If you pause, dither or dawdle you could permit agitation and worry to occur concerning perhaps your derogatory predictions about the quality of future results. Therefore, if you want or need to pause, do it deliberately. Put your pencil down and take a soggy spaghetti arm rest. Working and playing speedily also includes doing things slowly as well as quickly. However, it does not mean being hasty. Remember the saying, 'less haste, more speed'.

> *The understanding which we want is an understanding of an insistent present. The only use of a knowledge of the past is to equip us for the present. . . . The present contains all that there is, it is holy ground; for it is the past and it is the future.*
>
> A.N. Whitehead

Rule V – Do much

If you do a lot of work, you are able to try many alternatives and produce a number of variations more easily. This rule helps you to become as flexible as possible. Also a large quantity of 'tryouts and attempts' at an early stage enables you to make clear choices later on. In other words, 'Do not put all your eggs in one basket'.

> *Drawing is a means of finding your way about things, and a way of experiencing more quickly, certain tryouts and attempts.*
>
> **Henry Moore**

Rule VI – Work and play concurrently

Working and playing concurrently complements Rule V. Rather than finishing one design completely and then moving onto the next, try working several designs concurrently; because you are able to discover new things every time you make a mark you will be able to transfer this element of knowledge to another design immediately and with ease by applying this rule. You can watch all of your designs growing and developing together. With regular practice you should find this rule very useful and you can apply it to other exercises in this book, indeed use it with other activities in your life. You probably do anyway. Have you ever found in your work and play a certain problem occurring which seems insoluble? Have

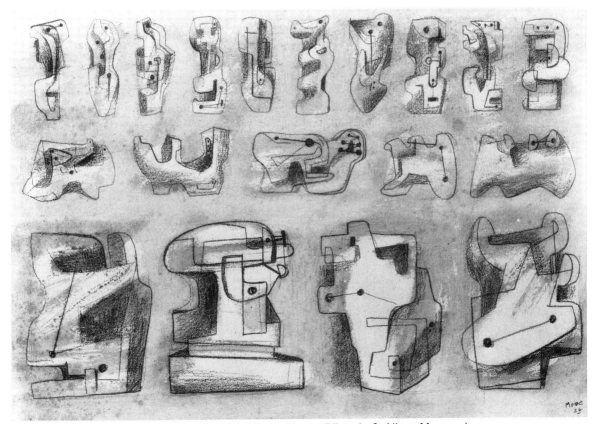

Fig. 11 — Studies for stone sculpture, 1936. *Henry Moore (Victoria & Albert Museum)*

you also found that however hard you try at the time you cannot solve it, but if you leave it for a while and then return the answer has appeared in an instant. I find this when I do not seem to remember the name of someone I know quite well! Although it is important not to run away from problems altogether (remember the 'giant'), it is also important to understand that it is often necessary to leave the problem for a while, particularly if it has been worrying you for some time. Indeed, your resulting worry often leads to a dislike and even a hatred of what you have been doing. Thus, this rule allows you to move quickly to a new design and return to previous ones well before such detrimental thoughts are permitted to occur. This rule can be summarized by the statement, 'A change is as good as a rest'.

12b

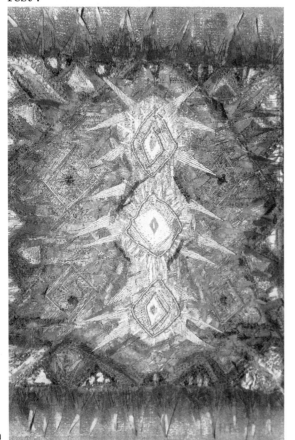

12a

Fig. 12a, b, c — *The value of exploring a number of possibilities around a central theme.*

The three embroideries illustrated here are all by Hilary Bower. You will find what she says about her work useful and interesting:

'For quite some time I have drawn my inspiration from architecture. That is to say the decorative aspects such as archways, vaulting, plasterwork and the many shapes and combinations of decoration. I also love Indian and Islamic art and textiles and I think that a long period of admiration for them naturally finds itself feeding into my work. The quality of old tapestries and well-worn fabrics and embroideries also inspires me, and it is this quality which I try to incorporate into my work. Hence the frayed and worn edgings on some of my work.'

'My starting point is to draw and photograph those objects and shapes within the buildings which catch my eye. I then develop these by introducing collage and a variety of media. It is when the strong shapes, marks, patterns and differences of surface texture begin to emerge that I know it is time for translating the paper idea into textiles. I try to keep my work "free" and to preserve and enhance the marks and

12c

lines I have made with paint and pencil in my embroidery. It is these qualities which I feel express my work and are often the essence of it. The way in which I tear the paper for the collage is the way in which I try to cut the fabric.'

'Recently I find the introduction of other elements such as hand-made paper, paint and crayon within the embroidery itself interesting. A moulding and a blending together of these with fabric, stitchery and threads is inspiring and challenging.'

Rule VII – No adverse criticism.

This rule is probably the most difficult to apply, but it is also the most important and most useful. If you apply all the preceding rules to your work and play, you will find this easier to fulfil. This rule should not be confused with the necessary activities of clear assessment and positive evaluation of what you do and how you do it. It means simply not disliking what you do and certainly not denigrating your designs and how you produced them. Remember such ideas are the unnecessary burdens for this, your voyage of discovery.

These are the seven main rules by which this game may be played with ease. Furthermore, these seven main rules govern *all* the exercises in this book. Apart from one or two exceptions in some of the subsequent exercises these seven rules will remain constant.

At this point you can now start to practise the activities of assessing and evaluating. Assessment is being able to see what has been done. Evaluation is being able to see the value of what has been done and forecasting its use, where appropriate, in the future. So, return to your 12 rectangles and without any derogatory criticisms assess how you have brought into play a combination of similar elements and opposing or complementary elements when you have read the next paragraph.

> *Art is harmony. Harmony is the analogy of contraries – the analogy of similarities, of tone, of colour and of line.*
>
> **Georges Seurat**

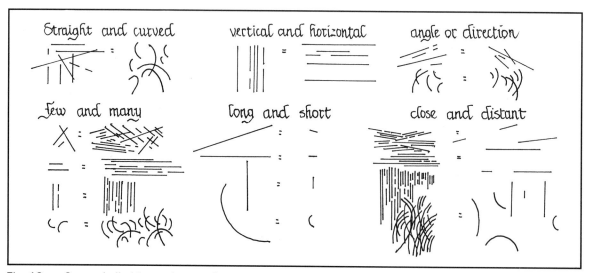

Fig. 13 — *Some similarities and contraries or complementaries of line.*

14

Figs 14 and 15 — *The value of contrary, complementary and contrasting elements as agents in composition and harmony. Figure 14 shows a jacket (detail) c.1985, photographed by Jessica Stray. Figure 15 shows* Phrases from my Life, *1986. Both these embroideries are by Julia Caprara. Observe what she says about her work and compare this with the precepts contained within Seurat's statement (p. 38) and also within Matisse's statement (p. 130).*

'My work evolves from a series of apparently contrasting events and often very varied forms and qualities. The "poem" or poetic response to outside phenomena is developed parallel with an intellectual and analytical breakdown of the event and evolved together with symbols or "sounds" from the unconscious, triggered by these vibrations, the synthesis of the "makings" creates through the image the visual event or celebration of life.'

'The jacket was worked by both hand and machine embroidery, using a wide variety of yarns, threads and fabrics, such as ribbons, laces and silks in order to create a "light-modulating" surface, but my main concern is with contrast. I usually employ only two stitches, the button-hole and the french knot. I like the idea of a limited vocabulary to develop a wide contrast by varying the sizes, proportions and forms of the circular unit.'

15

'Phrases from my Life *is composed of wrapped threads, using machine embroidery threads. Each unit is made separately and then assembled later with hand stitchery to create one whole textile surface. Each unit or wrapping is composed with those colours which I am "in tune" with at the moment. (I usually work in the car – I can't stand being passive on any journey!) Each group becomes a phrase and one "sound" from my life.'*

One important aspect of designing is how similar and complementary elements are balanced and harmonized, such as straights and curves, verticals and horizontals, long and short, large and small, thin and thick, many and few, high and low, left and right and so forth. Very often a solution to a problem about a design which seems unbalanced lies in bringing into play similar elements or complementary elements with those that seem to be causing the problem. For example, if your design is composed of diagonals lying all in one direction, try including some lying in the other direction. For another example, if the shapes, which have occurred by your interacting lines, are all about the same size and seem too repetitive, try drawing more intersecting lines which are closer together in one area only so that you create a balanced contrast of large and small. Look at the illustrations on p. 42 and notice how such problems have been observed and attempts to solve them have been tried in this way.

Now take up your pencil again and continue to develop your designs in this way by including more similar elements and those which are opposite or complementary. Remember to proceed as before by using the seven rules to guide you. This part of the exercise should take about ten to fifteen minutes. This includes the final stage when you need to make the start and finish of every line touch either another line or one side of the rectangle so that all the resulting shapes are self-contained and whole. The reason for this will be clear when you do the next exercise on tone and shading.

When you finish, put your design sheet away in a drawer or a folder. Bring it out again later, perhaps the next day for your next assessment of this first part of the game. Try to remember that you will not know what your designs will look like until they are completed. Thus, there is no purpose in assessing or judging them finally until they are finished. Just as a jury must hear *all* the evidence before they can come to a verdict so also must you have all your information. Moreover, this really needs to be done in a cool detached manner rather than in the heat of the moment. This is why I urge you to put your design sheet away and look at it tomorrow.

You need to do plenty of these design sheets in order to try many variations. You may not be feeling tired now, so do another right away. If you are feeling a little exhausted you should pursue another activity altogether and return to this later.

Draw twelve more rectangles, as before, on a fresh sheet and keep a wider margin between each rectangle than before. This allows you more room to write a few notes under each design like those in the illustrations. Next choose to limit the categories of lines you will use, such as verticals and horizontals, or curves, diagonals and verticals. Then proceed in exactly the same manner as before but make some definite decisions before you draw your lines, like drawing just a few of one type of line and many of another; or drawing your lines closer together somewhere near the centre and further apart at the outer edges of the rectangle. Look at the illustrations to help you and note how it is possible to make quite marked differences by an apparently slight change in either amount, proportion, position or direction of line. Before, during and after you draw your lines, write under each design some brief notes about your preliminary decisions and any change of plan while you are doing them as in Figs. 16a and b.

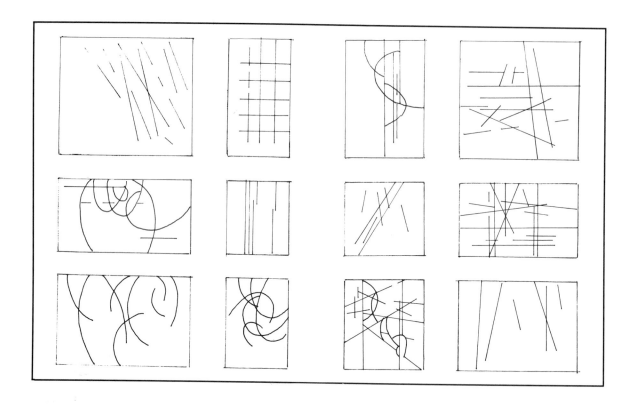

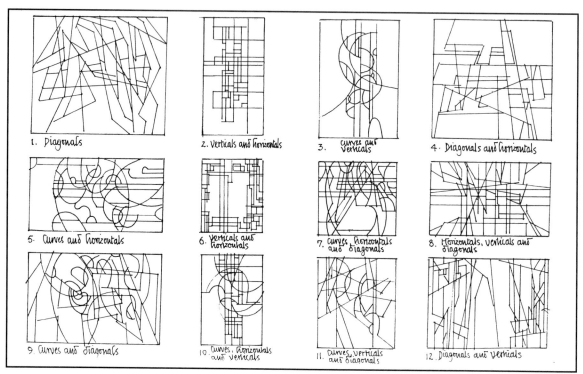

1. Diagonals

2. Verticals and Horizontals

3. Curves and Verticals

4. Diagonals and Horizontals

5. Curves and Horizontals

6. Verticals and Horizontals

7. Curves, Horizontals and Diagonals

8. Horizontals, Verticals and Diagonals

9. Curves and Diagonals

10. Curves, Horizontals and Verticals

11. Curves, Verticals and Diagonals

12. Diagonals and Verticals

16a

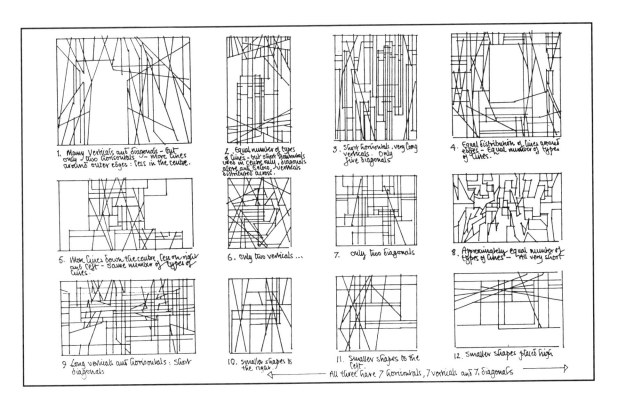

Fig. 16b — *Variations of the use of verticals, horizontals and diagonals.*

(1) Many verticals and diagonals, but only two horizontals. More lines around outer edges: less in the centre.

(2) Equal number of types of lines, but short horizontals used in the centre only, diagonals above and below, and verticals distributed from top to bottom.

(3) Short horizontals, very long verticals, only five diagonals.

(4) Equal distribution of lines around edges. Equal number of types of lines.

(5) More lines down the centre, less on right and left. Same number of types of lines.

(6) Only two verticals.

(7) Only two diagonals.

(8) Approximately equal number of types of lines. All very short.

(9) Long verticals and horizontals: short diagonals.

(10) Smaller shapes to the right.

(11) Smaller shapes to the left.

(12) Smaller shapes placed high above.

Sketches 10, 11 and 12 have seven horizontals, seven verticals and seven diagonals

Fig. 16a

(1) Diagonals.
(2) Verticals and horizontals.
(3) Curves and verticals.
(4) Diagonals and horizontals.
(5) Curves and horizontals.
(6) Verticals and horizontals.
(7) Curves, horizontals and diagonals.
(8) Horizontals, verticals and diagonals.
(9) Curves and diagonals.
(10) Curves, horizontals and verticals.
(11) Curves, verticals and diagonals.
(12) Diagonals and verticals.

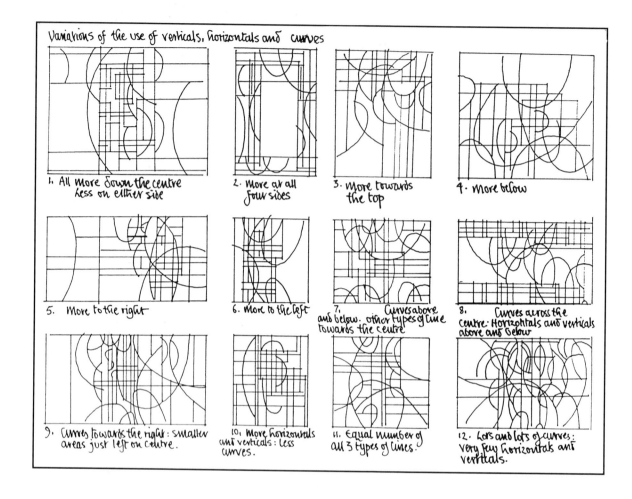

Fig. 16c — *Variations of the use of verticals, horizontals and curves.*

(1) *All mainly down the centre. Less on either side.*
(2) *More at all four sides.*
(3) *More towards the top.*
(4) *More below.*
(5) *More to the right.*
(6) *More to the left.*
(7) *Curves above and below other types of line towards the centre.*
(8) *Curves across the centre. Horizontals and verticals above and below.*
(9) *Curves towards the right. Smaller areas just left of centre.*
(10) *More horizontals and verticals. Less curves.*
(11) *Equal number of all three types of lines.*
(12) *Lots and lots of curves. Very few horizontals and verticals.*

When you bring all of your design sheets for assessment and evaluation a few days later, continue to assess and evaluate within the terms of harmony and balance which you have already practised. There is also *another set* of terms by which you can make assessment. Respond to your designs in terms of the *mood* they convey to you, but before you assess your own, look at the next set of illustrations and respond to the arrangements and compositions of lines in terms of moods or feelings. Included in these illustrations (Fig. 17a-e) are some responses by others. Notice that they are not all quite the same but many fall within a similar category. How do your responses compare with these by other people?

When you have made your own assessment of the illustrations in terms of mood, then try to guess what the subject might be. The compositions of lines are actually taken from paintings and embroideries. Notice the wide range of subjects which other people have thought the lines to represent. These you will find next, placed upside-down, so you can guess the subject *before* being influenced by others! Now look at the illustrations at the end of the chapter in order to check your responses with the originals on pages 77, 78, 79 and 80 (Figs. 29a, b, c, d and e).

Have you noticed how most people's responses often match the artists' intentions in terms of mood and feeling whereas the subject has not always been guessed correctly? Even when quite different moods have been stated, as in the case of the El Greco painting (Fig. 29e), several moods have been represented quite deliberately. The diagonals on the left indicate a restless outward movement of the traders and the curves on the right indicate the restful stability of the disciples. Have you noticed the medallions at the top on the picture? Another expulsion scene is shown on the left: Adam and Eve are being driven from the Garden of Eden. And another depiction of trust is shown on the right: Abraham is sacrificing Isaac.

Many artists, craftsmen and designers have been, and still are, aware of how all the formal elements of line, tone and colour can be chosen and arranged quite deliberately to represent feelings and moods. Read Seurat's statement below and observe how this can be so.

> *Cheerfulness of tone is the bright dominant; of colour, the warm dominant; of line, lines above the horizontal. Tranquility of tone is equality of dark and pale; of colour, of warm and cold, and the horizontal for lines. Melancholy of tone is the cold dominant, and of line the downward direction.*
>
> **Georges Seurat**

Now look at your own designs and make a clear assessment in terms of the moods and feelings they convey to you. Try to remember Rule VII – no adverse criticism! If you dismiss any of your designs because you do not like them, you may be in danger of ignoring some important advantages; for example, it may be that very kind of 'disliked' angry and aggressive arrangement of lines will convey just the emotion that you will need to express in an embroidery one day.

At this point you have completed the first part of this game.

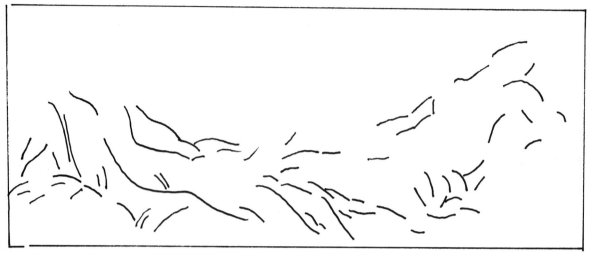

a

Fig. 17a, b, c, d, e — *Responses in terms of mood and feeling.*
(a) Relaxed, peaceful, languid, heavy, quiet, tired, gentle, tranquil, slow, flowing, secure and safe.
(b) Spiky, sharp, aggressive, noisy, violent, offensive, oppressive, stinging, shrill, biting, alert, painful, quick, tense and dramatic.
(c) Swinging, graceful, awkward, flying, confusing, quarrelsome, buoyant, glowing, majestic but also pugnacious.
(d) Happy, joyful, cheerful, jubilant, soaring, sunny, merry, glad, warm, enjoyable, amusing, embracing and comforting.
(e) Right – *stable, quiet, pensive, thoughtful and loyal.* Left – *unsteady, precarious, sudden, mobile, excited, alive and speedy.* The whole – *stately, authoritative, proud, calm and magnificent.*

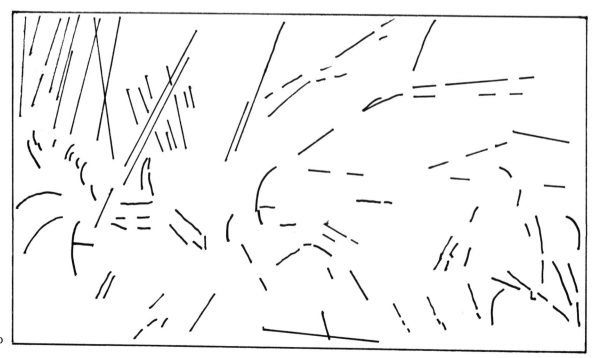

b

c

17d

17e

Key to Fig. 17 – Responses in terms of subject matter

(a)   Tree roots
      Landscape
      Mountains
      Reclining figures
      Flowing stream

(b)   Storm in the forest
      Ships on a rough sea
      Earthquake
      Battle
      Leaves blowing in a strong wind

(c)   An old-fashioned fairground swing
      A large bird sitting on rough water
      St Christopher
      A vase of dead flowers
      Two people quarrelling on a park bench

(d)   Sunshine through clouds
      A breezy day
      Trees in springtime
      Angels singing
      People talking and laughing together

(e)   In the underground
      Shopping in a supermarket
      Street scene
      Crowded room
      People in church

51

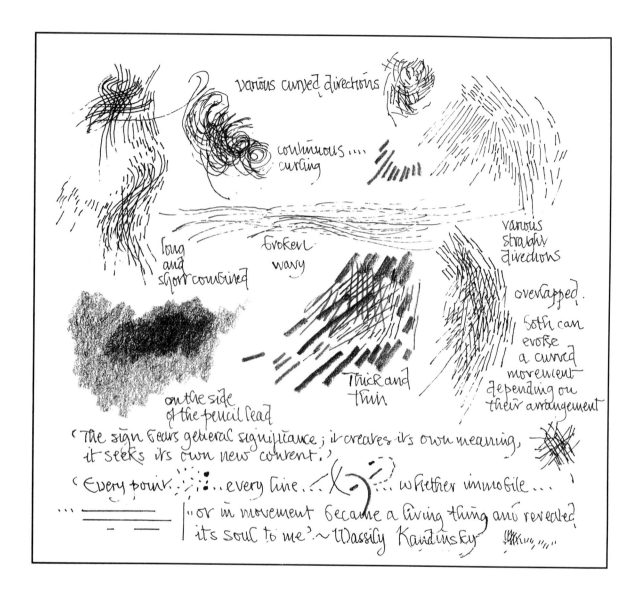

various curved directions

continuous .... curling

long and short combined

broken wavy

various straight directions

overlapped.

Both can evoke a curved movement depending on their arrangement

on the side of the pencil lead

Thick and thin

'The sign bears general significance; it creates its own meaning, it seeks its own new content.'

'Every point ... every line ... whether immobile ... or in movement became a living thing and revealed its soul to me'. ~ Wassily Kandinsky

Exercise 5 – Shading with ease

Practise both the soggy spaghetti arm and the golden cord exercises. Then, pin a fresh sheet of paper to your drawing board and try using your pencils in various ways in order to make lots of shading marks. Try to proceed in the same way as you did while you were practising your sheet of the senses in Exercise 3. In fact, this is another sheet of the senses, but which concentrates on tone. Try to remember to write notes as you proceed as in the illustration. Always use the seven rules to help and guide you so that you continue to play this enjoyable game with ease and delight. Look at Fig. 18 to help you to do this. Also look at Figs. 19a, b and c, to help you realize how all this is pertinent to both drawing and embroidery.

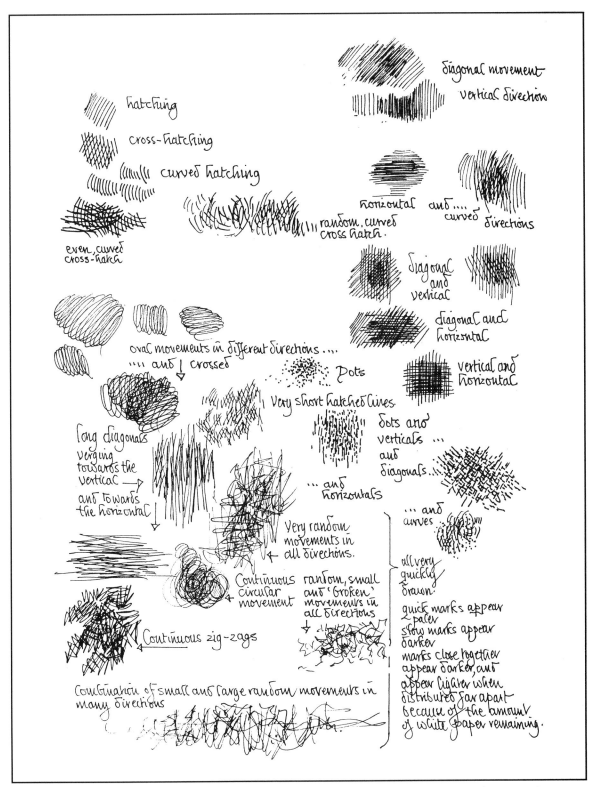

Fig. 18 — *Various ways of shading. Tone is the range between light and dark; tint is a pale tone and shade is a dark tone.*

Fig. 19 — *The value of tone and direction of marks as elements of compositional structure in drawing and embroidery.*

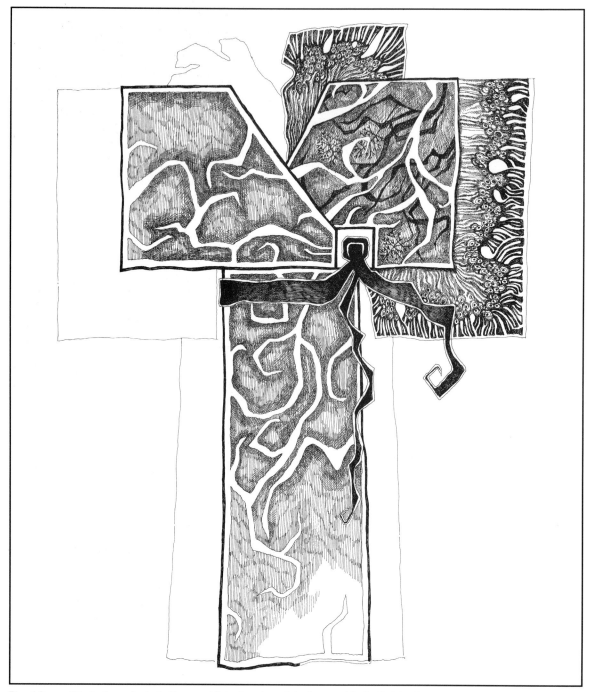

Fig. 19a — Study for a jacket. *Pen and ink drawing (black on white), Robin Giddings, 1985.*

Observe how the subtleties of the close tones have been realised by cross hatching techniques and how the interplay of the various line directions help to integrate the drawing as one whole pattern.

54

Fig. 19b — Panel (?) for a screen. *Linen embroidered with thick, soft, twisted silks (ivory, coral, peach, rust, three light greens, pale blue and pale yellow). Design by William Morris. Either executed by his firm or supplied by them in kit form. Late nineteenth century. (Collection of the Embroiderers' Guild)*

Observe how a very sensitive gradation of tones is apparent with the range of pale tints, and how this contrasts with the occasional dispersal of darker shades at certain, appropriate intervals. Notice also how the pattern of directional darning stitches assists the integrity of the design.

Fig. 19c — Landscape. *Jan Beaney, 1981. Photographed by Dudley Moss. (Collection of Mr and Mrs Curtis)*

Observe how the balanced contrast between two main types of stitch help to make a unity of the embroidery as a whole.

Jan Beaney has always been inspired by light effects, tonal conditions and the changing qualities of land and seascape according to the weather.

'I am fascinated by the play of light on the surfaces. More recently I like to interpret in fabric and thread the images found within rock faces along with the subtle colour and tonal variations caused by ever-changing light conditions.'

Exercise 6a – Tones without tears

Practise the restful exercises; pin a fresh sheet of paper to your drawing board and prepare a 2B pencil. You are going to follow a precise recipe by which you will be able to make a number of tones from light to dark with ease. Look at Fig. 20 to help you.

Stage 1

First of all, draw a small shape like a rectangle or a circle, about two or three inches big, somewhere on your paper. Divide this shape into nine sections. Choose one of these sections and mark it with the number *1*.

Stage 2

Then shade *very* lightly all of the sections except the one you have marked with the number *1*. This you leave white. To help you, try holding the pencil very lightly and listen to the pencil making a very quiet sound. Furthermore move the pencil across the sections as if they were one whole shape. This will help you to keep your shading even. If you shade each section separately, you will find it much more difficult to keep your shading even.

Stage 3

Next choose one of the shaded sections and mark it with the number *2*. Leave this and section *1* as they are. Shade the remaining sections together as before. Hold the pencil just a little more firmly and you could also change the direction of the pencil marks. Including the white section you have achieved three tones already.

Stages 4–9

Continue in this manner. At each stage choose another section to mark with the next number. Leave all the numbered sections as they are. Shade the remaining unnumbered sections together as if they were one *whole* shape. Change the direction of your shading and exert a little more pressure at each stage until you reach the ninth and last tone. When you have completed this, try different variations of the same exercise. Try different ways of shading such as dots or cross hatching. Try another pencil such as a 2H. You could change your drawing medium altogether and try a ball point or fibre-tipped pen. Try also shading more than nine sections. The more you do, the more you will discover and the more confident you will become. Look at Fig. 21 to help you.

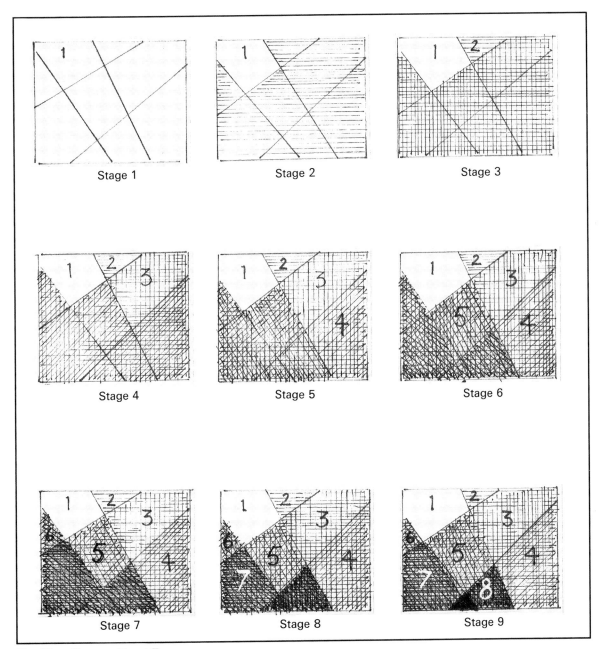

Stage 1   Stage 2   Stage 3

Stage 4   Stage 5   Stage 6

Stage 7   Stage 8   Stage 9

Fig. 20 — Tones without Tears.

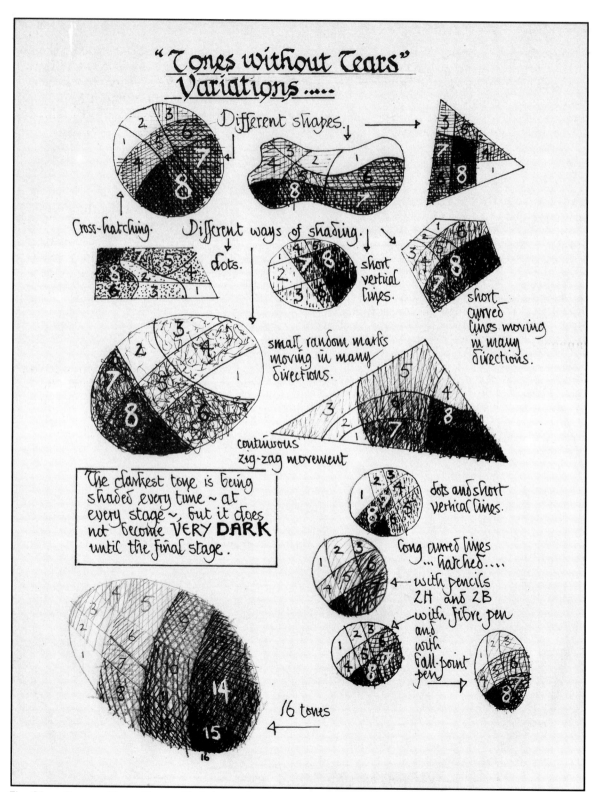

Fig. 21 — Tones without Tears – Variations. *The darkest tone is being shaded every time – at every stage – but it does not become very dark until the final stage.*

Exercise 6b – Tones with tears

In order to demonstrate how easy it is to achieve an even graduation of tones by the *tones without tears* method, try now this exercise, *tones with tears* and compare both methods with respect to their relative ease and difficulty.

Stage 1

Draw ten squares linked together in a horizontal format and number them above from one to ten as in Fig. 22a.

Stage 2

Begin your shading by leaving the first square the white of the paper and shade the second square the palest tone you can manage as in Fig. 22b. Mark these two squares with the numbers *1* and *2* below. This indicates the order in which you are doing them.

Stage 3

Then shade the tenth square the darkest tone which your pencil will allow. Make it as black as possible. When you finish, mark it below with the number *3* to indicate that you have shaded this third in the order of your doing them as in Fig. 22c.

Stage 4

The next square you shade is the sixth one. That is, the one which is placed half way between the second and the tenth square; you have to estimate the grade of tone that comes between them as in Fig. 22d. (N.B. You are *not* allowed to alter it later on!)

Stage 5

The next stage is to shade the fourth and the eighth squares and to estimate the tone that comes between the second and sixth squares, and the sixth and tenth respectively as in Fig. 22e. (N.B. No rubbing out!)

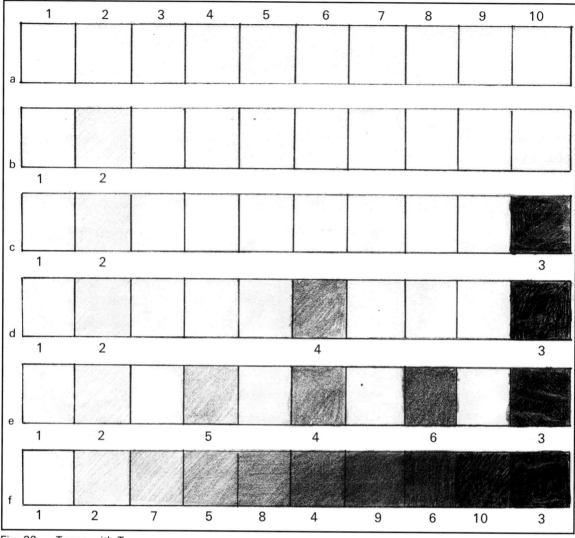

Fig. 22 — Tones with Tears.

Stage 6

The final stage is to shade the remaining four blank squares; namely the third, the fifth, the seventh and the ninth by estimating their relative tonal values compared with the others as in Fig. 22f. Now that you have completed this tones with tears exercise, compare its difficulty with the relative ease of the previous tones without tears exercise. Although it is very useful to do, my present concern is to keep the exercises easy and consistent for you for the duration of this book. Therefore, when you use tonal values for any of the subsequent exercises, I shall be asking you to transfer the principle and practice of the tones *without* tears method.

Exercise 7 –
Composing tonal harmonies

First practise the restful exercises. Then choose one of your designs that seems to work in terms of harmony and mood. Trace it and transfer many alternatives of this design on fresh sheets of paper. Try moving the design round 90° each time you transfer it and also try reversing the design to get a mirror image. In fact you have eight possible variations. Furthermore, you could enlarge or reduce the variations by photocopying. Look at

Fig. 23a, b and c to help you. Then choose one of your alternatives and use the following variation of the tones without tears method. Use Fig. 24 to help.

Stage 1

Choose as many or as few sections as you wish and mark these with the number *1*.

Stage 2

Shade all the remaining sections very lightly together as if they were one whole area. This will keep your shading even.

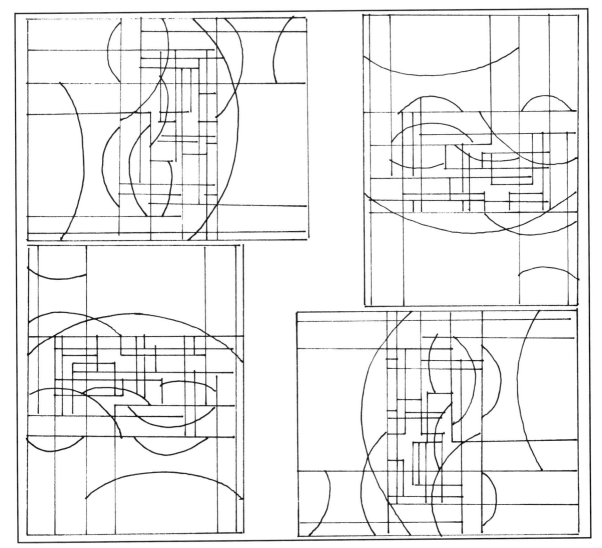

Fig. 23a

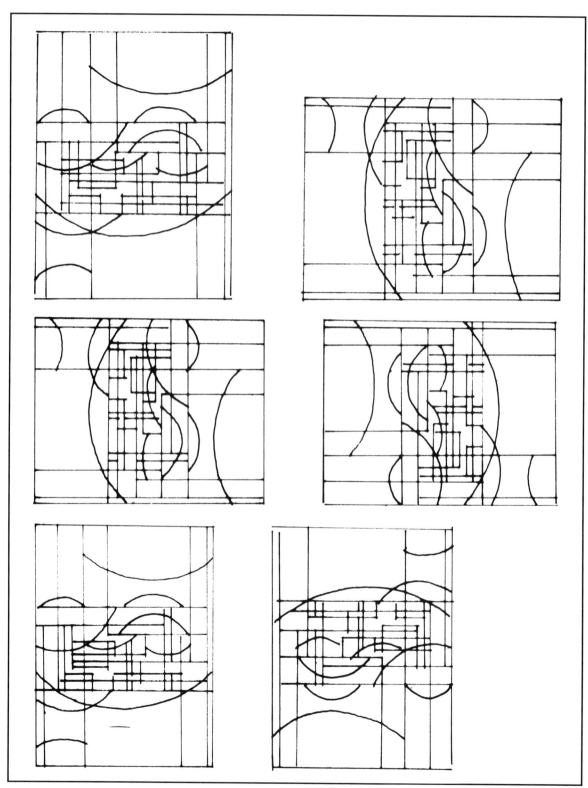

23b

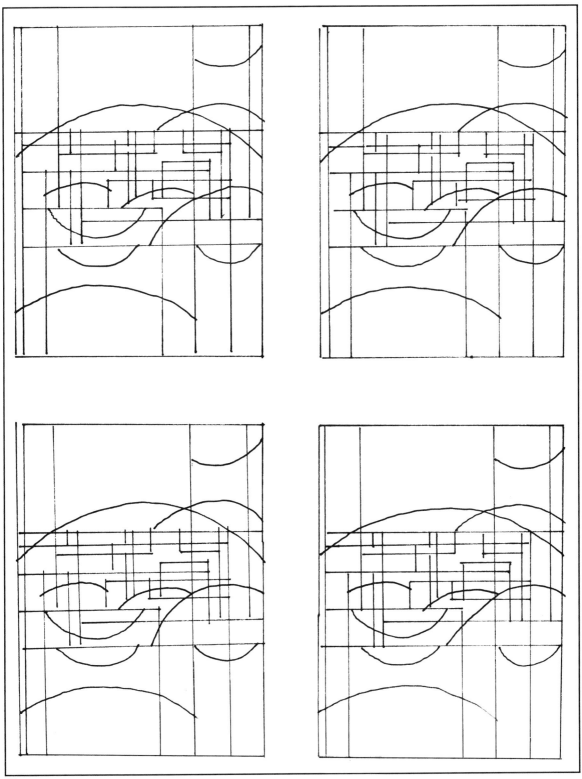

23c

Stage 3

Erase all of your number *1*'s within the white sections. Then choose as many or as few of the lightly shaded sections and mark these with the number *2*. Shade all of the remaining sections as before, leaving the white sections and those marked with the number *2* alone.

Stages 4–10

By now you can see that you are following the tones without tears method as before. The only variation is that you can choose how many or how few sections to shade at each stage. Therefore

continue in this manner until your pencil achieves its darkest shade. Soon you should discover that it will be unnecessary and even inhibiting to write the actual numbers within the sections you choose to leave, because you are beginning to understand the principle which determines this method of shading the design as a whole in stages.

The advantage of your seeing the *whole* design developing in tones from the very beginning is very important.

You can appreciate from the first tint you make how the design as a whole unit is shaping in terms of a balance of tones. This helps you to make a more reasoned

Fig. 24

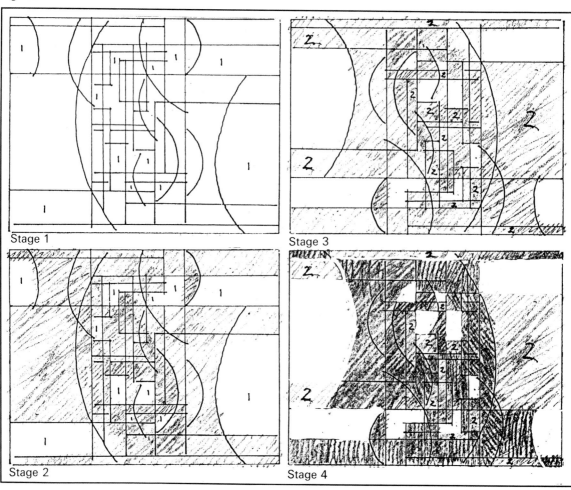

Stage 1

Stage 2

Stage 3

Stage 4

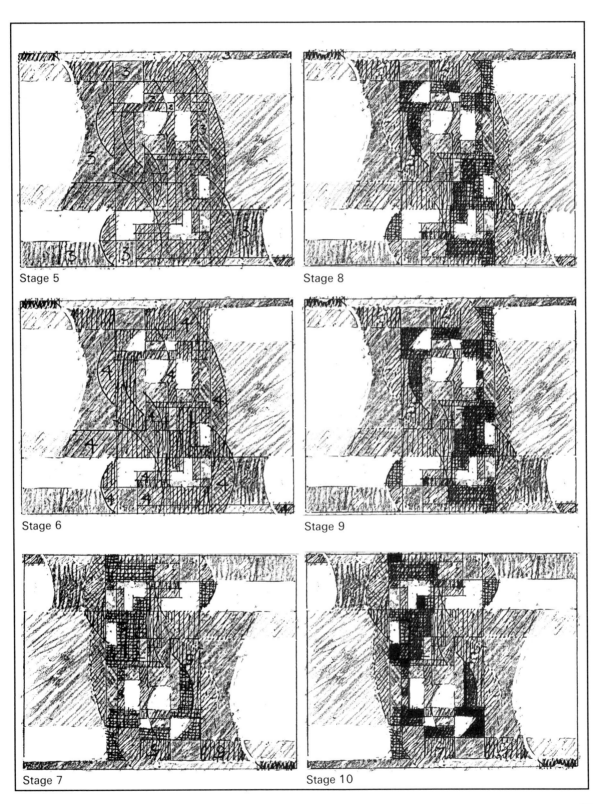

Stage 5

Stage 8

Stage 6

Stage 9

Stage 7

Stage 10

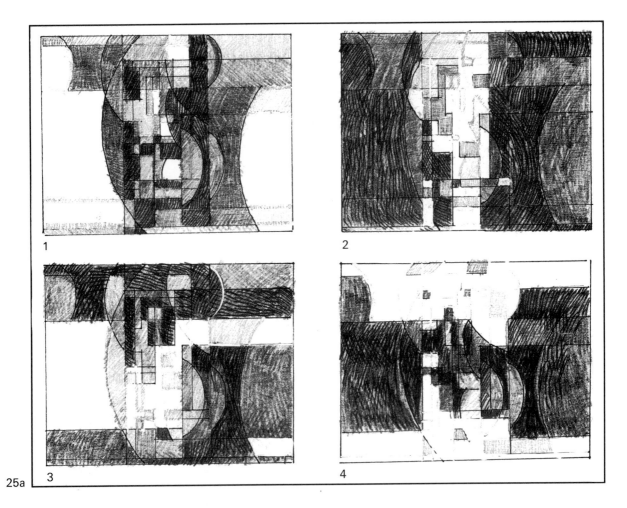

25a

and informed decision about where you place the next tone, so that you may achieve a harmony of similarities and contraries of tones.

You need to do plenty of variations just as you made lots of designs with lines and shapes. You will find this great fun to do and also you will have a number of completed tonal designs which you can assess and evaluate in terms of both harmony and mood as you did earlier with lines and shapes. Look at Fig. 25a, b and c to see the enormous variety of tonal compositions from just one design in lines and shapes. Notice also how different moods can be achieved by the use of tones.

Fig. 25 — *Variations of tonal harmonies.*

Fig. 25a — *(1) Dark tones mainly down the centre.*
(2) Light tones mainly down the centre.
(3) Light tones mainly across the centre.
(4) Dark tones mainly across the centre.

Fig. 25b — *(1) Light tones mainly on the right, left and down the centre.*
(2) Dark tones mainly on the right, left and down the centre.
(3) Mainly dark tones to form a cross shape.
(4) Mainly light tones to form a cross shape.

Fig. 25c — *(1) Light tones mainly at the top left and bottom right.*
(2) Dark tones mainly at the top left and bottom right.
(3) Dark tones mainly at the right of centre.
(4) All mainly light tones.
(5) All mainly dark tones.
(6) Light tones mainly below centre.

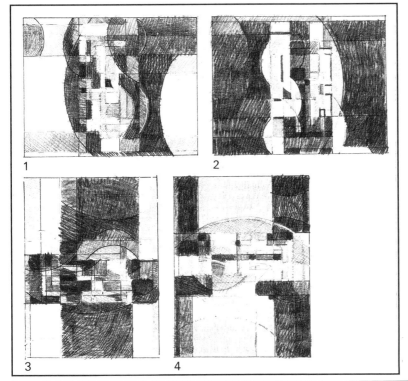

1

2

3

4

25b

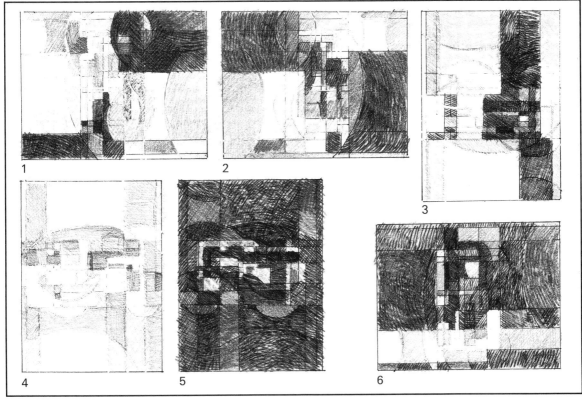

1

2

3

4

5

6

25c

Try to remember to put all seven main rules in practice so that your designing becomes easy and fun to do.

Now, having said that, you are ready to *bend* some of the particular rules for this exercise because you understand the principles which govern them. For example, do please add or remove one or two lines in each design as you proceed with your shading if you think this helps to balance the design more effectively. Alternatively, when you have made your darkest tones at the end, you may need to re-establish some light tones again with an eraser for the same reasons of balance and harmony.

Thus, try to understand that the rules for any particular exercise in this book are here to help you, not to impede you. On the other hand the seven main rules (pp. 34, 35, 36 and 38) still need to be observed faithfully.

Fig. 26a — *An example of crewel work embroidery where chain stitch has been used throughout, by Jean Mooney. The design was developed after attending a 'Design for the Nervous and Anxious' course in 1986.*

Fig. 26b — *Detail of a canvas embroidery panel worked with white wools by Mariel Stapleton as a result of attending a similar course in 1985.*

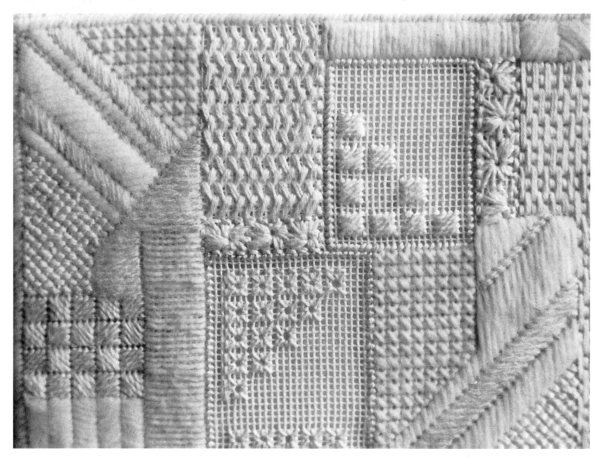

Fig. 26c — *An example of blackwork embroidery by Jennie Parry from a design made during a course in 1986.*

Fig. 27 — *The value of detail in design.*

'By river's shadowed light grow the wild blooms of midsummer'. *Embroidery, Verina Warren 1985.*

'Detail and design have always been strong influences on my work. My developing interest in landscape has provided greater contrast for this detail, seen against much larger open flat areas of colour. In design, contrasts are seen again, landscape within landscape and season within season, whilst technically developments have been the juxtaposition of painting with embroidery and the use of silk-bound borders in linking these elements together.'

The design was taken from a watercolour drawing which forms the central section. It was worked out on graph paper to help the structure and proportion of the main shapes of both the central section and the border. Colours are then air-brushed on silk fabric except for the mid and far distant areas, which are painted by hand to suggest depth. Hand embroidery with straight stitching is then worked over the colour in order to achieve a light surface texture. The machine embroidery stage is very fluid and flexible allowing the colour to develop spontaneously within the design. The outer border is also air-brushed and then painted with acrylic. Its purpose is both to emphasize the central landscape and to extend the design outwards. The wrapped silk borders define the two adjacent surfaces, while their colour has the effect of connecting them.

Exercise 8 – Colour experiments with ease

Now you are going to play with colour. First of all practise the restful exercises. Then clip fresh sheets of white cartridge paper to your drawing board and have the following coloured pencils on the table near you. You need two reds, two blues and two yellows. Look at colour plate 1a(1)–(6) so that you can match those in the illustration.

This is probably the easiest way to select your coloured pencils because there are many suppliers who call the same colours by different names. Of the reds you need one that looks close to orange. This is sometimes called scarlet. You also need a red that looks close to purple. This is often called crimson. Of the blues you need one that looks close to purple. This is often called ultramarine. You also need one that looks close to green. This could be a cobalt or a cerulean blue; it could even be turquoise. Of the yellows you need one that looks close to green. This is sometimes known as lemon yellow. You also need one that is close to orange. This could be a gamboge or a chrome yellow.

Colour is for many the most alluring and attractive of all the formal elements. In order to enjoy colour fully it is necessary to discover some of its simple laws and so find pleasure in all of its myriad complexities.

> *Everything comes from everything and everything is made from everything and everything can be turned into everything else; because that which exists in the elements is composed of those elements.*
> **Leonardo da Vinci**

Understand that all colours belong to each other and can harmonize with each other. Physical scientists have discovered that they are all components of white light.

It might come as a surprise to you, as it did at first to me, that the average person can distinguish between 120 and 200 individual colours. Perhaps this explains the variety of opinions about how many 'pure' or 'main' colours there are in the spectrum. Nine, seven, and six colours have all been suggested. For our purposes we shall remain with six main colours. Look now at colour plate 1b(1), (2) and (3) and observe how the two reds, the two blues, and the two yellows are arranged to create a circle and also mixed one with another to produce purple, green and orange. Now make a colour circle in this way on your sheet of paper.

Now you have the six main colour hues. Red, blue and yellow are known as the primary colours. Purple, green and orange are known as the secondary colours. The word 'hue' is used to describe the quality that distinguishes one colour from another. Furthermore, colours that lie opposite to each other within the colour circle are known as complementary colours. Thus, red is complementary to green, as is blue to orange, and yellow to purple. Now look at colour plate 1c(1), (2) and (3) and try, yourself, surrounding each colour with its complementary and then by each of the two colours which are next to it within the colour circle. These are known as adjacent colours. Can you see how the colour 'inside' seems to change? The juxtaposition of complementary colours seems to enhance the power of both colours, whereas the juxtaposition of adjacent colours seems to subjugate their powers and make them seem more gentle.

Now look at colour plate 1d(1) and (2) and take just one of your coloured pencils like the hue of blue that is close

71

to purple, as in the illustration, and practise the tones without tears method. Now, do it again but mix with the blue at each stage that hue of red which is close to purple so that you achieve a range of tones with this secondary colour, purple. Try this with as many colours and mixtures of colours as you like. This will consolidate your understanding that every hue of every colour can be made light or dark. In terms of colour this is known as value or tonal value.

Now look at colour plate 1e and make another colour circle, but this time make and place the palest tones (the tints) of all the colours at the centre and grade them so that you achieve their darkest tones (the shades) at the outer edges of the circle.

Now, choose one of the six main colours within the circle, like green for example. Take the two hues of yellow and the two hues of blue (that is, the primaries which make green – a secondary colour), and try to make as many variations of green as you can. Look at colour plate 2a–f and use it to help you make as many hues, tints and shades as possible. Notice that such procedures as your choice and number of hues of colours, the order in which you choose to overlay each on the other and the amount of each hue are the means by which you can achieve all these subtle variations. Have you also noticed that although the illustrations show as many as 36 different greens, there are many more combinations and permutations by which still more variations might be achieved?

All colours come from white light – black is the absence of light. Greys, browns and blacks can also be made by mixing colours together. Look at colour plate 3 and notice how browns can be made in different ways. The main principle to understand is that if you mix the three primary colours, all these can

be achieved. As you continue to look at the illustration, you can notice how, as before, your choice of particular hues combined with others will produce different results. It is also possible to overlay complementary colours to produce similarly varied results. If you refer back to your colour wheel you can see that a mixture of a pair of complementaries is in fact another way of mixing the three primaries. Now enjoy making as many different browns as you can.

Now look at colour plate 4 and notice how the appearance of grey and black, as well as brown, can be achieved. This depends on how little and how much colour is used.

Look carefully at this illustration and, at the same time, follow these next directions so that you can do this variation of the tones without tears method yourself.

Stage 1(a)

Draw a rectangle and divide it into seven sections. Take a blue pencil and shade all the sections very lightly.

Stage 1(b)

Take a red pencil and shade all the sections very lightly over the blue.

Stage 1(c)

Take a yellow pencil and shade all the sections very lightly over the blue and red.

Stage 1(d)

Choose one section and mark it very lightly with the number *1*.

Stage 2(a)

Leave the section marked with the number *1* alone. Lightly shade the remaining six sections with the blue first . . .

Stage 2(b)

then with the red . . .

Stage 2(c)

and lastly with the yellow.

Stage 2(d)

Choose another section and mark it with the number *2*.

Stages 3, 4, 5 and 6

Continue in this manner. Each time choose another section to mark with the next number. Leave this and all the previously numbered sections alone. Shade the remaining unnumbered sections in the same order of colours as before. Each time you shade treat the remaining sections as if they were one large section. In this way your shading will be more even. Also try to change the direction of your shading and exert a little more pressure at each stage until you reach the sixth and the seventh tone. Look now at colour plate 5a–g where you can see that it is possible to make many variations of tones and also of hues of greys, browns and blacks. This depends on which particular hues of the three primary colours are used. Try now making a number of variations yourself.

Look again at colour plate 5a–g and observe how some of these browns could be interpreted as dark tones of primary and secondary colours. For example, 5a could be darker tones of blue and 5g could be darker tones of green. Now look at colour plate 6a–f that emphasizes this point. The six circles of colour appear like three-dimensional spheres with a part of each in shadow. This is achieved by using only the three primary colours in each one. The wording for the illustrations indicates that those colours that are underlined are used first and the remaining colours are used for the shadow. Now try this yourself.

At this point you have practised *all* of the main colour experiments that you need for all of the remaining colour exercises for the remainder of this book. Try to practise them many times; first, for fun, secondly to give you confidence, and thirdly so that you may more easily transfer such methods later on.

Fig. 28 — *Bayeux, 1984, Jean Littlejohn. A blend of images from Bayeux worked on felt and muslin layers with applied lace and scrim. The threads used include Madeira Burmilana, Madeira Metallic Supertwist machine embroidery threads, and some hand stitching has been worked in Madeira Six Strand Embroidery Floss.*

Exercise 9 – Composing colour harmonies

Now you are going to have fun employing some of the colour experiments from the previous exercise, with your original design and make colour harmonies.

As always, first practise the restful exercises, then transfer lots of variations of your original design on fresh sheets of paper and pin these to your drawing board. Take up the same six coloured pencils as before (that is, the two hues of each of the three primary colours) and also a green, an orange and a purple. Now that you have understood how you can make these secondary colours from the primaries you are ready to make even more subtle variations.

Look at colour plate 7a(1)–(2) to help you. Choose one colour only. One hue of green was used for the first illustration. Try making as many tints and shades of green as you can by employing the tones without tears method with this one coloured pencil. Remember that *all* these colour exercises employ the principle of the tones without tears procedure.

Next take the coloured pencils that are adjacent to your chosen colour. The next illustration was made with the two hues of yellow (lemon and chrome) and the two hues of blue (cobalt and ultramarine) together with the original green. Now compose a harmony of tints and shades of several hues of green.

Now look at colour plate 7b(1)–(2). Choose a pair of complementary colours; hues of red and green were used for these variations. Also hues of blues and yellows were used with the green. You can choose any pair you like. In time, try playing with all three pairs. The first illustration shows how mainly reds and their pale tones are placed down the centre and dark greens are placed either side. In order to create another balanced contrast, a few greens are brought into play down the centre and a few reds on either side.

The second illustration shows how greens and reds are dispersed more evenly over the whole composition, and the dark tones are down the centre and the light tones are placed either side.

Try now exploring what you can do with complementary colours.

Now look at colour plate 7c(1)–(4). These four illustrations are a reinterpretation in colour of the tonal exercises shown in Fig. 25a. Only the six original coloured pencils have been used. Here various hues of blue, yellow, red, orange, purple, green, grey, brown, and the appearance of black can be shown to contribute to one composition – thus emphasizing Leonardo's statement on page 71.

Try as many variations and series of variations as possible. When you finish each group put them away for a while. Practise the same kind of procedure in assessing and evaluating your work as you have done before. Bring your designs out in a few days' time, lay them all out before you and regard them in terms of how you have balanced and harmonized the similarities and contraries of line, tone and, now, colour.

You have already discovered that you can assess and evaluate your design only by observing the relations between one thing and another and also by their relation with the composition as a whole. Thus, it is only when all the elements such as shapes, tones and colours come together, as they always are together in nature, that you can assess and evaluate your own designs in terms of total harmonious compositions.

> *That each part has its own particular arrangement is not enough; they must all agree together and make but one harmonious whole.*
>
> **Roger de Piles**

Try to remember that each and every part of your design is a true and valid member of your entire composition.

> *The parts of it being so connected that if any of them be either transposed or taken away, the whole will be destroyed or changed; for if the presence or absence of something makes no difference it is not part of the whole.*
> Aristotle

Do you remember how you played the game concerning moods and emotions with lines, and how you played the same game with your designs composed of tonal harmonies? Now you can play the same game with your colour harmonies. Read Georges Seurat's statement again on page 47 and also the following two statements. Then respect your own work in this way.

> *Colours though less diverse than lines, are nevertheless more explanatory by virtue of their power over the eye. There are tonalities which are vulgar, harmonies which are calm and consoling, and others which are exciting because of their boldness.*
> Paul Gauguin
>
> *Harmonies and concords of colours which are sufficient in themselves and which succeed in touching us, to the depths of our being; without the aid of a more precise or clearly enunciated idea.*
> Claude Monet

Now you have done this without any adverse criticism (remember rule VII) but in a truly objective and discerning manner, you can rest in the knowledge that you have enjoyed observing yourself discovering wonderful things about the natural elements of line, shape, tone and colour. It really does not matter whether your results are good or bad. What is far more important at this stage is how sensitively aware you have been and are still becoming.

> *Sensitivity to nature must come first: technique does not matter.*
> Paul Cézanne
>
> *There is nothing either good or bad but thinking makes it so.*
> Shakespeare – Hamlet

The miracle is this. You will find that if you attend to the sensitive observing process you will discover that many splendid designs arise as a rewarding consequence.

> *Proper attention to the finishing, strengthening, of the means, is what we need. With the means all right, the end must come.*
> Swami Vivekananda

Fig. 29a — Venus and Mars. *Sandro Botticelli, c.1445–1510. (National Gallery)*

Fig. 29b — The Rout of San Romano, *Paolo Uccello, c.1397–1475. (National Gallery)*

Fig. 29c — The Syon Cope. *Detail – St Michael slaying the dragon. Thirteenth century, English. (Victoria & Albert Museum)*

Fig. 29d — The Adoration of the Shepherds. *Inscribed on the back 'Edmund Harrison imbroiderer to King Charles made theis Anno Dom 1637'. (Victoria & Albert Museum)*

29d

Fig. 29e — Christ driving the Traders from the Temple. *El Greco, c.1541–1614. (National Gallery)*

Chapter Three

DRAWING FOR THE TERRIFIED

Many years ago when I had finished teaching a day-school on design for one of the branches of the Embroiderers' Guild, I was approached by the programme secretary who asked me what other courses I did. 'I could do one on drawing,' I replied. 'Oh! but we are all terrified of drawing,' was the immediate response. I had already suspected for some time that there were many people, and embroiderers in particular, who would really like to be able to draw but who were also too scared to start and even more afraid to join a drawing class because of their feeling of inadequacy and their suspicion that all the other students would be better than they; this would increase their terror even more. As a result I have used the title 'Drawing for the Terrified' for nearly all my courses for beginners. Luckily it seems to encourage the nervous and anxious prospective drawers to come along and have a go. Maybe they all thought to themselves, 'Well, we shall all be in the same boat!' In a way this was true; they were all embarking on a voyage of discovery just as you also have been discovering something about designing and are now about to discover something about drawing.

Whether or not you believe this now, it is important that you consider the fact that given a functioning mind to think, eyes to see and limbs to make marks with, everyone is capable of drawing. (Incidentally I use the word 'limbs' because as you probably know some people with no arms or hands can draw with their feet and others with their mouths.) Like language and numeracy the potential to draw is innate in all human beings. If evidence is needed, you need only to look at the drawings of young children from about the age of 2 years and onwards. Uninhibitedly and confidently they begin to scribble and then to develop a system of marks which soon evolve into elaborate schemata which represent their responses to the world around them. Look at Figs. 30a–g to see how quickly this system is developed.

> *To create form is to live. Are not children who conceive directly and from their secret feelings more creative than those who imitate Greek art? Are not savages who have their own form, strong as the form of thunder? Man externalizes his life in forms. Every art form is the externalization of his inner life. The external appearance of a form of art is its inwardness.*
>
> **August Macke**

Unfortunately, this innate potential has been impeded for many adults, mainly for a number of environmental reasons. Fortunately it can never be destroyed, although it may appear so. The fact of the matter is that it is only hidden. So rest assured, those of you who think it has gone for ever.

The term drawing has had many

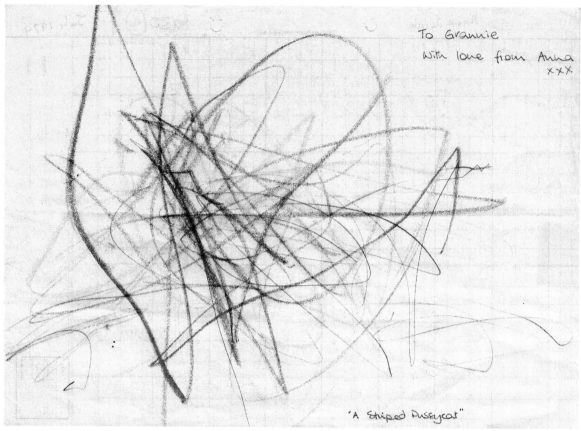

To Grannie
With love from Anna
x x x

"A Striped Pussycat"

30

Fig. 30a-g — *These are all drawn and painted by Anna from the age of 2 to 8 years. Reproduced by the kind permission of Barbara Buttle, Anna's grandmother.*

different meanings at different times and in different places. Indeed it still does. There are many ways to draw and all of them are right and correct. Every designer, every craftsman and every artist chooses particular and varied ways of drawing which are appropriate and necessary for each unique mode of expression. However, for the time being and for the purposes of this book, I propose in this chapter to show you just *one* way. I want to help you draw what you see, as you see it, in terms of line, tone and colour. Furthermore, in order to keep everything as simple as possible for you, I shall be showing just a *few*

particular approaches and procedures to help you to begin to achieve this way of seeing and being able to draw what you see.

You may know of a book called *Drawing on the Right Side of the Brain* by Betty Edwards; this not only proves the theory that everyone is capable of drawing but also shows how you can do it in practice. Because this book is so useful I have decided to adapt and use two of the exercises here to begin with. Both of these exercises show you that if you can learn to 'see' clearly you *will* be able to draw what you are looking at.

30b

30c

30d

30e

30f

30g

Exercise 10 – The upside-down drawing

First of all prepare yourself by practising the soggy spaghetti arm and golden cord exercises, so that you become relaxed but also alert and attentive. Then clip a piece of paper set vertically on your drawing board and have a 2B pencil sharpened in readiness. Look now at Fig. 31 which is an upside-down and simplified version of

Fig. 31

The Sketch of the Artist and Head of Ugolino by William Blake.

Start by looking at the upside-down drawing and become aware that what you are really seeing is an arrangement of many different kinds of lines. Now look at just one line and notice whether it is long or short, and whether it is straight or curved. If it is straight, ask yourself, 'Is it a vertical or a horizontal or a diagonal?' If it is a diagonal, ask yourself, 'In what direction does it lie?' Perhaps the line you are looking at is curved; if so, ask yourself, 'Is this curve open or is it a closed curve?' Whatever kind of line it is, also ask yourself, 'Does this line touch or overlap another line, and how far or how close is it to another line?' Now ask yourself, 'What kinds of other lines lie above and below this line and what kinds of lines lie to the right and to the left?' Look then at the drawing in terms of just the kinds of lines by which it has been composed *rather than* seeing it as a representation of a head with a face and his features. This is why the drawing has been turned upside-down.

Now start drawing one of the lines that you see somewhere at the top of the upside-down drawing on your paper in a position that is approximately the same. Then draw the next one to it, and then another and again another. As you do this keep *thinking* in terms of the type of line you *see* and allow your pencil to record that type of line you see. Above all, avoid trying to name parts of the head and face like m-o-u-t-h or n-o-s-e. If you do slip into this way of thinking you will probably frighten yourself and think, 'I can't draw mouths and noses!', and as a result you may avoid drawing these represented parts altogether. Therefore, try not to make things difficult for yourself by conjuring up such 'giants'. Please believe that this exercise is as simple as just drawing the lines as you see them.

Although you need to make every attempt to record each line as accurately as you see it and to place all other lines in the same relation to each other, please do not be overconcerned if you do not always achieve this exactly as you wish. This will happen later with much practice just as the novice piano player may not always play the right notes at first, but will be able to do so in time. Therefore do not erase or correct any of your lines but continue forward at a relaxed but speedy pace. If at any time you feel tense or worried, just put your pencil down and have a soggy spaghettiarm rest for a few seconds and then continue to draw in a relaxed but attentive manner until you record the very last line and thereby finish the drawing. Remember also that the third of the main rules for *all* the games in this book (page 34) is to help you to come back to the present if your mind has been wandering. Try to remember to listen to the sound of your pencil working and to feel its touch as it gently moves as well as looking at the drawing.

When you have drawn all the lines and, thus, completed your drawing, then turn both drawings the other way round. You should be very pleased with the way you have managed this. As this is your first attempt, you may not have drawn all the various lines in proportion with each other; perhaps they are too wide or too long apart. Never mind! Remember that this is your first attempt and you need to congratulate yourself on how you have managed to record *all* the information as accurately as you are able. Remember also that the beginner piano player is not able to play all the notes in Schubert's *Impromptu in A Flat* correctly the first time it is played! Next time and, with more practice, all the next times you will be able to judge your proportions more precisely.

When I do this exercise on my

'Drawing for the Terrified' courses, I put the upside-down drawing in an envelope so that the students have no knowledge at all about what the drawing might represent. I ask them to pull the drawing out of the envelope an inch at a time and to draw the lines as they see them at every stage. About half way they eventually recognize that the drawing represents a head and the most common reaction is that of momentary terror! However, they very soon realize that if they continue trusting in the lines themselves just as they did before, all will be well. Indeed, a few without terror have persevered in the belief that all is well. All (so far) have continued to finish the drawing with ease.

If you like, why not ask a friend to put a simple line drawing in an envelope so that you do not know what the representation is and which will compel you to draw it in this way? Do try it, it is great fun to do.

Once you have become used to this way of seeing and thinking choose a more complex drawing. You could choose one with tone and later on a coloured drawing. Although it would be unwise to rely *only* on copying other people's drawings, it is a most useful way of learning how they respond to nature and of learning different ways and methods of mark making. If you do this in conjunction with your own drawings it can help you to see the world with new eyes and help you to develop your own systems of drawing directly from nature.

Now you are ready to play the next game, after which I shall explain, in terms of how your brain works, why you managed this upside-down drawing with such ease.

Exercise 11 – The profiles

Start as always by practising the soggy spaghetti arm and golden cord exercises so that you may become relaxed and attentive. Then clip a piece of paper onto your drawing board and have a 2B pencil sharpened in readiness. You will now need to read both of the next two paragraphs before you begin so that you understand all the instructions.

Begin drawing an imagined profile of a human face on the left side of the paper looking towards the centre. (If you are left-handed you will need to draw this profile on the right side of the paper facing the other way so that it too is looking towards the centre.) Start at the top of the paper with the forehead and continue with all the features such as the eye-socket, the nose, the lips, the chin and finish with the neck which needs to touch the bottom of the paper. Draw this profile in one continuous line. As you draw, listen to the verbal instructions in your head which you will need to give yourself in order to do this drawing. You will discover that you will find it necessary to *name* the different features of the face because your drawing is of an imagined profile. Allow this naming to happen.

When you have completed this profile, look at it carefully and draw it again on

 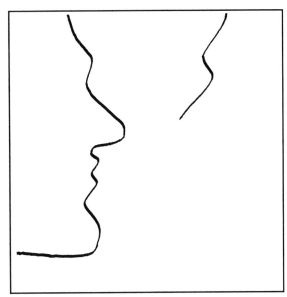

Fig. 32 — *(a) For those who draw with their left hand. (b) For those who draw with their right hand.*

the other side of the paper as exactly as you can, but this time draw it in reverse. Produce a mirror image. Try to match all the different kinds of contours that you see in the first profile and draw them the other way round. As before, listen to the instructions in your head which you need to give yourself in order to do this drawing. You will find that these instructions will not be the same as before, but I do not want to state yet what these might be because I would like you to observe them for yourself; we can discuss them after you have done the drawing.

So, do the drawing now and do not read any further until you have finished both profiles.

Now that you have completed drawing the two profiles, compare the two sets of 'instructions', which you had to give yourself. They were not the same, were they? Whereas it was necessary for you to name every feature in turn while you were drawing the first, imagined, profile, you found it unnecessary, even

impossible, to use names while you were drawing the second profile. You may not have used words at all. This is because your instructions were concerned with estimating different kinds of contours and angles, various lengths of directions, and how each part of this second line related spacially to the first line.

Embodied in this exercise is the most crucial message and underlying principle for observational drawing. It has also been important for the games you have already played with designing. As you read on you will begin to understand how relevant it is.

You may be aware already that your brain is divided into two parts, or, as they are more properly known, two hemispheres. The left hemisphere is constructed in such a way that it understands words, sequences, numbers and time. It is logical, analytical and rational. Complementary to this, the right hemisphere has a minimal connection with words, sequences, numbers and is unaware of time. However, it is constructed in such a way to be spacial, holistic and intuitive. That is, it understands how things are related to each other spacially; it can see whole things all at once, and can also make leaps of insight.

This is just a very brief synopsis of the functioning of the two hemispheres of your brain. If you want to know more, then I suggest you read the first few chapters in Betty Edwards' book, *Drawing on the Right Side of the Brain* from which this and the previous exercises have been adapted. For the time being and for our purposes I believe I have given you enough theoretical information.

If you now think back to how you managed the upside-down drawing you will realize now how it was necessary to do it with the use mainly of your right hemisphere. Do you remember that if you started to name certain features it not only started your rational, left hemisphere working with questions, it also, in those few moments only, actually prevented you from *seeing* the lines as they actually were?

Look back again at the quotation on page 34 and recall how our perceptual make-up prevents us from being able to attend fully to more than one message entering any one sense channel at any one time. Now look at the drawing of your two profiles again. You may have noticed already that sometimes you see a vase and sometimes two profiles. Look at the drawing again. Perceive the vase first and now perceive the two profiles. Now try perceiving them simultaneously. You cannot do this, can you? You are, however, aware of a vase with space either side at one moment, and the next moment you are aware of two profiles with a space between them.

Many of us have been unaware of how precisely our perceptual mechanism does actually operate. Because of this, we have often tried and failed, by employing

the inappropriate hemisphere for a certain task. This is often the reason for so many people believing that they are incapable of drawing from observation. It is because they have tried to use the left hemisphere to do the right hemisphere's work. The logical reasoning, rational questions have actually prevented their right hemisphere from operating and observing spacial relationships. If they allow it to do so then they will be able to learn to draw from nature with ease just as you have started to do. There is more truth in Michelangelo's statement than a first reading might make apparent. You now understand that the emphasis is really on learning how to 'see'.

> *What your eye can see your hand can draw.* **Michelangelo**

You are now ready to play the next game.

Exercise 12 – The handkerchiefs

As always prepare yourself by becoming relaxed and attentive with the soggy spaghetti arm and golden cord exercises. Clip a fresh sheet of paper on your drawing board and sharpen both a 2B and a 4B pencil in readiness. Now read and follow these next directions carefully.
1 Make a slope on your table. This can be done easily by resting a flat object like a large book onto a pile of smaller books. The slope should be about 30°.
2 On this slope place a sheet of white paper as in Fig. 33a.
3 Spread out a white handkerchief on the paper.
4 Then take another white handkerchief and arrange this in a multiple of folds and creases and place this on the first handkerchief as in Fig. 33b.

a

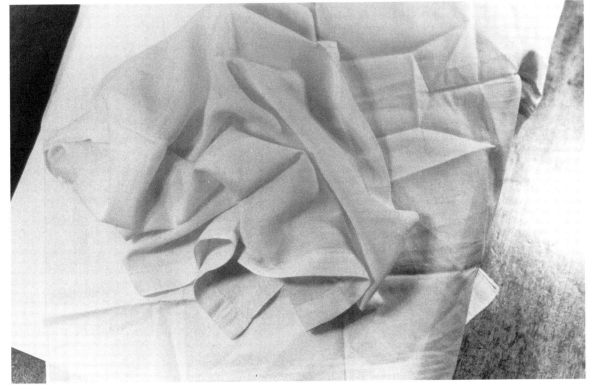

b

Fig. 33

33c

5 Next make two right-angled corners cut from card in the form of the capital letter 'L' about 15cm (6in) high and wide and clip these together so that you form a rectangle as you see in Fig. 33c. Notice that you can alter the size and proportions of this rectangle in as many ways as you like. This is now going to act as your 'viewfinder'.

6 Now place your viewfinder onto the handkerchief arrangement so that you see just a part of the folded handkerchief and some of the first handkerchief behind it as in Fig. 33c.

7 You will need to set the whole arrangement so that the light comes from either the right or the left. This will allow for many variations of tones to be achieved ranging between some very light ones and some very dark ones. You might even place a table lamp on one side so that the shining light will provide this effect for you very distinctly as in Fig. 33c.

You have now set up your still-life. Allow yourself to become still and quiet once more, particularly if your left hemisphere has been annoying you with tiresome questions like, 'I'm not going to draw anything as complicated as that, am I?'

Then allow yourself to look at everything you see in your viewfinder. Avoid naming or analysing anything such as, 'There is a folded handkerchief on top of another one spread out underneath it'. Allow your right hemisphere to operate and *see* what you are looking at in terms of the variations and range of tones. Your left hemisphere understands the edges and contours of the folds because your right

92

hemisphere perceives the sudden or gradual differences in tonal values. Do not yet be concerned with drawing, but simply enjoy looking at the amazing variety of tones.

> *I would rather teach drawing that my pupils may learn to love nature, than to teach the looking at nature that they may learn to draw.*
>
> **John Ruskin**

Now read John Ruskin's statement very carefully and notice now the emphasis is not so much on the *drawing as a finished result*, but rather on the *action and process of drawing*. You have already experienced that it is necessary to *see* in order to draw; now you are not only going to experience this again, but also how the action and process of drawing will help you to *see* even more and this will help you to 'love nature' even more.

One of my students said in an agitated manner before she began this exercise, 'What's *natural* about a boring old handkerchief?' She was, at that point, being directed by her left hemisphere only. However, she started to draw and as she persevered she became noticeably quieter and more peaceful, but at the same time, completely absorbed in her drawing. When she had finished she said 'Although my drawing isn't in proportion yet and it doesn't really look like a handkerchief, while I was doing it I forgot what it was and really enjoyed trying to draw all those amazing tones. I realize now that I was really seeing and drawing the *natural* elements of light and shadow. Aren't they wonderful?' By this time she was being directed mainly by her right hemisphere.

Before you begin drawing look back at the tones without tears exercise (Fig. 20, p. 57) because you will be transferring that method of shading progressively and consistently from light to dark for this drawing; it would be helpful for you to do this exercise again somewhere on your paper to refresh your memory.

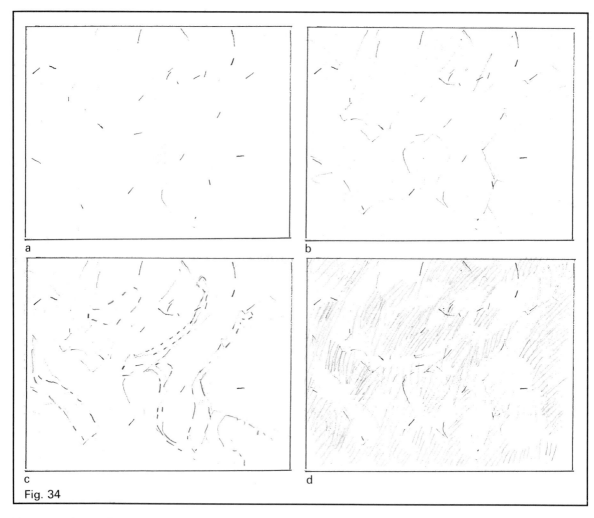

a

b

c

d

Fig. 34

Now read the following instructions
and as you do look at the illustrations,
Fig. 34a–1, to help you.

Stage 1

Start by drawing a rectangle on your
paper which is in the same proportion as
the inner confines of your viewfinder.
You may like to make it slightly bigger.
Many people seem to find it easier to
draw arrangements of objects like this
slightly larger than they perceive them.

Stage 2

There are two main reasons for using a
viewfinder. One reason is to help you to
find your view. This you have done. The
second reason is that you can use the
vertical and horizontal sides of the
viewfinder by which to measure and to
judge proportions. For example, you
should be able to see some very
distinctive edges and contours in your
view. One of these may touch or meet the
top horizontal of your viewfinder. Now,
ask yourself, 'Where, approximately, does
it "meet" this horizontal? Is it about half
way along, or is it a third or a quarter?'
Now notice at what angle this edge lies

34

as it continues across your view. You can estimate its angle approximately by comparing it with the same top horizontal of your viewfinder. Ask yourself, 'Does it lie to the right or to the left? Is it about 45° or is it less or more?' Continue to look at all those distinctive edges which you see within your viewfinder in this way. Simply enjoy estimating and judging the position, length, angle and type of contour by comparing it with the four sides of the viewfinder and with the other contours which you see.

Stage 3

Now take up the 2B pencil and as lightly as you can draw some broken or dotted lines that represent and record those same distinctive edges which you see in your view as in Fig. 34a.

Stage 4

Then take the same pencil again and confirm these broken or dotted lines with more assurance but still keep your lines very pale. Adjust, alter and amend them whenever necessary. There should be no need to erase any yet because your marks are very pale still. These pale marks act

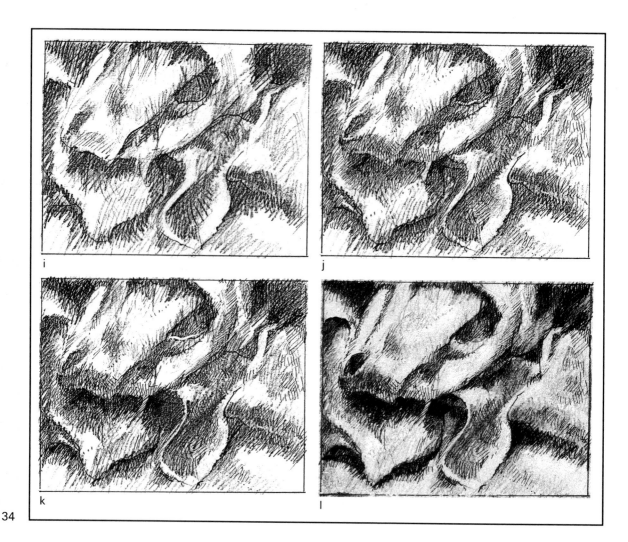

34

as your guide lines and structural foundation for the rest of your drawing as in Fig. 34b. One small boy who attended my Saturday morning art classes for primary school children said, 'It's like scaffolding, isn't it?'

Stage 5

Now half close your eyes and compare all the various tones which you see. Compare and contrast them with each other. Some are very light, some are very dark and there are many in between. Now discern those that are lightest of all.

For a minute transfer your thinking to your logical left hemisphere and say to yourself, 'If these parts are lightest of all then all other parts must be darker.' Remember this but now transfer your thinking to your right hemisphere and draw the outer edges of these lightest parts so they are established on your paper more distinctly. Look at Fig. 34c and note that these marks are still quite pale and you could still draw broken or dotted lines so that you allow yourself 'room' and the chance to adjust and correct whenever necessary.

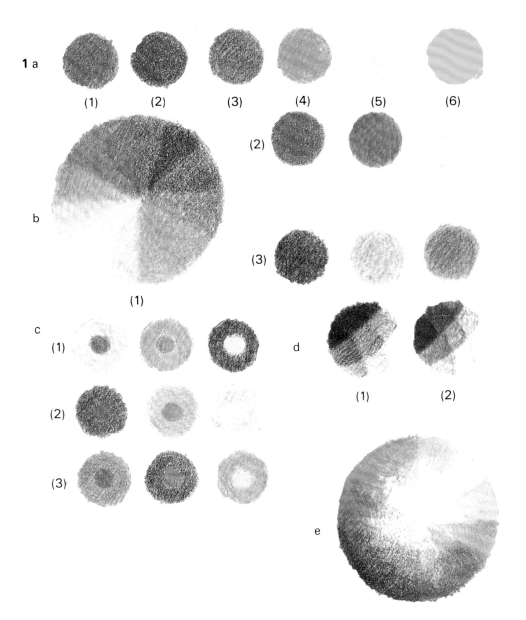

1a(1) *orange-red (scarlet)*
  (2) *purple-red (crimson)*
  (3) *purple-blue (ultramarine)*
  (4) *green-blue (cobalt)*
  (5) *green-yellow (lemon yellow)*
  (6) *orange-yellow (chrome yellow)*
  b(1) *The colour circle including two hues of each of the six main colours in the spectrum.*
  (2) *Red, blue and yellow are the Primary colours.*
  (3) *Purple, green and orange are the secondary colours.*

c(1) *The juxtaposition of primary colours with their complementaries, and (2) and (3) their adjacent colours.*

d(1) *'Tones without tears' with a hue of blue, and (2) with a hue of purple.*

e *Tints and shades of the six main colours within the colours circle.*

2a *Progressing from a little to a lot of lemon yellow and from a lot to a little of cobalt blue.*

b *Progressing from a little to a lot of chrome yellow and from a lot to a little of ultramarine blue.*

c *Progressing from a little to a lot of lemon yellow and from a lot to a little of ultramarine blue.*

d *Progressing from a little to a lot of chrome yellow and from a lot to a little of cobalt blue.*

e *Progressing from a little to a lot of lemon and chrome yellow and from a lot to a little of cobalt blue.*

f *Progressing from a little to a lot of lemon yellow and from a lot to a little of cobalt blue and chrome yellow.*

3 *Various browns made by overlaying different combinations to the two hues of each of the three primary colours.*

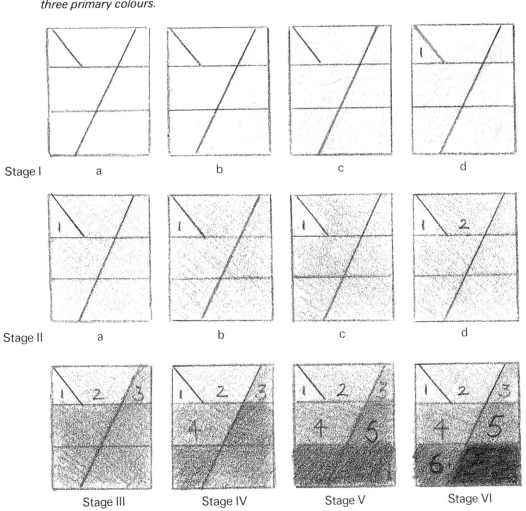

Stage I   a   b   c   d

Stage II   a   b   c   d

Stage III   Stage IV   Stage V   Stage VI

4 *Coloured tones without tears.*

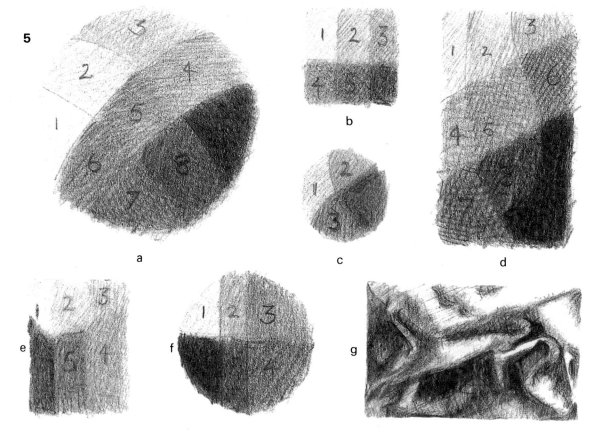

5 *Variations on the 'coloured tones without tears' method to achieve the appearance of greys, browns and black by using different combinations of hues of the three primary colours.*

a *Ultramarine, lemon yellow and crimson.*

b *Lemon yellow, cobalt blue and crimson.*
c *Chrome yellow, cobalt blue and scarlet.*
d *Ultramarine, lemon yellow and scarlet.*
e *Cobalt blue, crimson and chrome yellow.*
f *Ultramarine, chrome yellow and crimson.*
g *Crumpled handkerchief, Jo Pickering, 1986.*

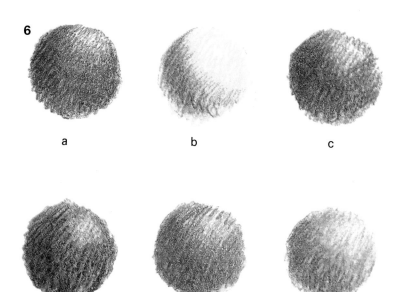

6a ***Red*** *with yellow and blue*
b ***Yellow*** *with red and blue*
c ***Blue*** *with yellow and red*
d ***Red and blue*** *with yellow*
e ***Yellow and red*** *with blue*
f ***Yellow and blue*** *with red*

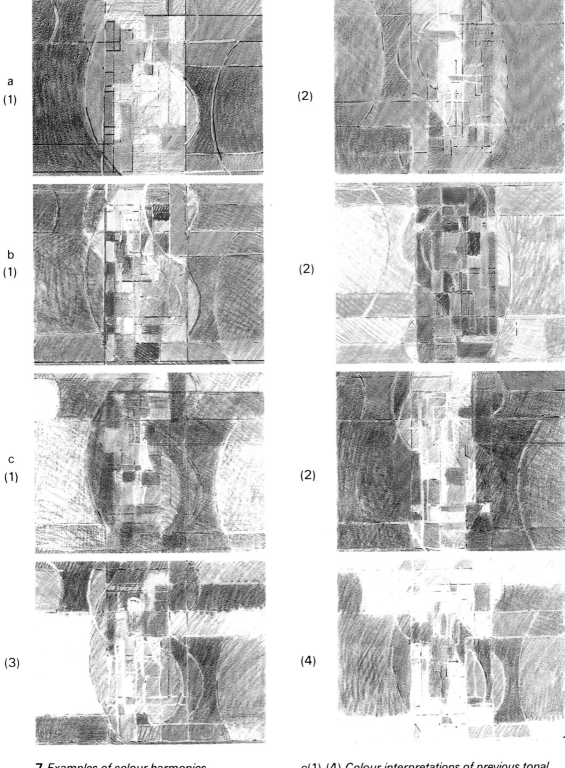

7 *Examples of colour harmonies.*

a(1) *Tints and shades of one hue of green.*

(2) *Tints and shades of several hues of green.*

b(1) *Reds and pale tones mainly down the centre.*

(2) *Equal distribution of reds and greens. Dark tones down the centre.*

c(1)-(4) *Colour interpretations of previous tonal compositions (colour plate 7) using two hues of red, blue and yellow.*

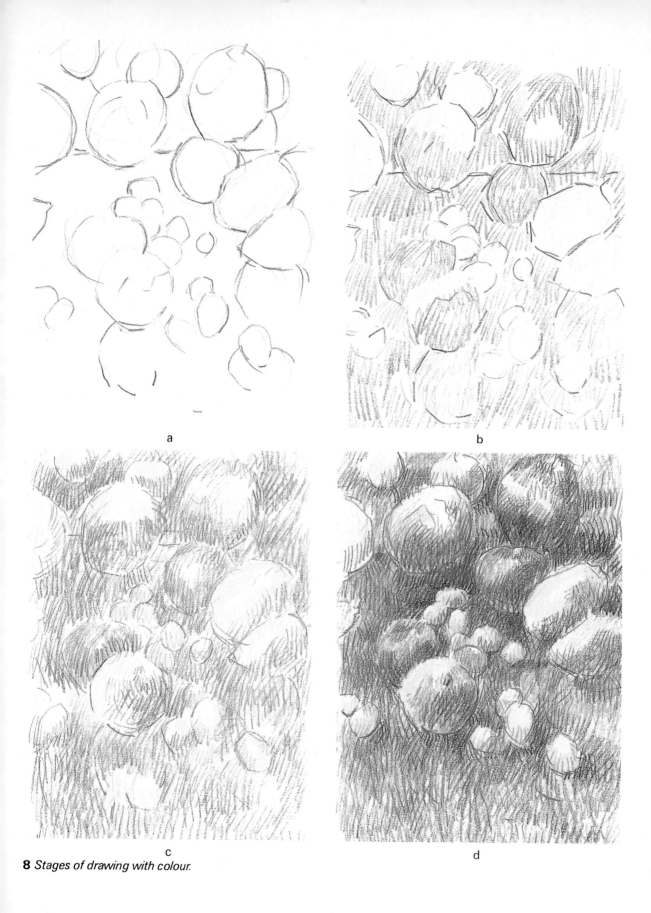

a

b

c

d

8 *Stages of drawing with colour.*

9a Delphiniums. Oil painting, Richard Box, 1979.

b Delphiniums. Embroidery, Richard Box, 1979.

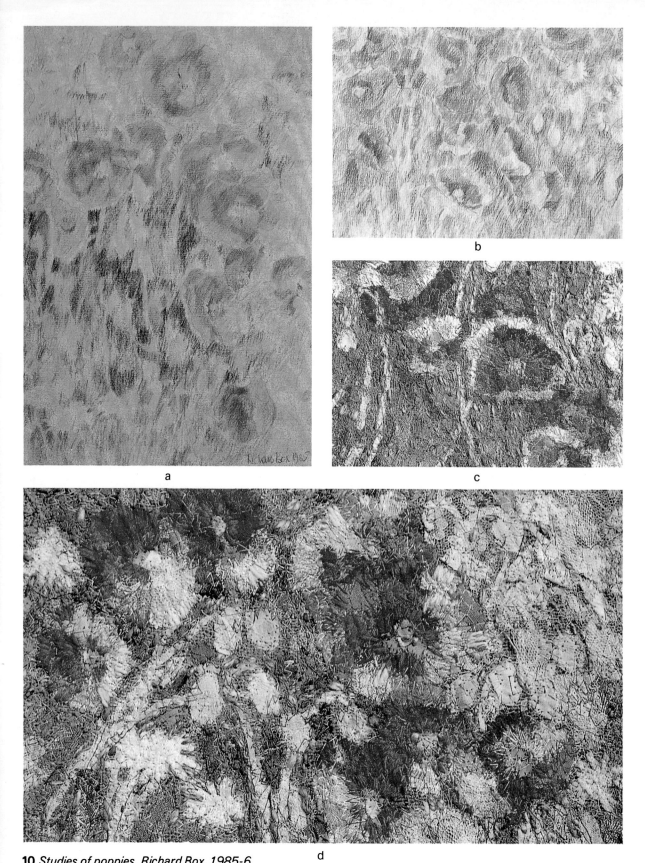

a

b

c

d

10 *Studies of poppies, Richard Box, 1985-6.*

Stage 6

Now shade all the other parts of your picture and keep those areas that you have established as being the lightest the white of the paper. Shade all the other parts as evenly as you can and as if they are one whole continuous part, as indeed, in terms of a total composition, they are. Keep your shading marks very pale. As you shade, keep looking most of the time at the view you see in your viewfinder. Can you see that the shadows seem to 'move' across the forms in different directions? Allow the pencil marks of your shading to move in the same directions as in Fig. 34d. Try to avoid shading all in one direction. A difficulty often created by some people is when they start drawing; the subject is given only a cursory glance and then their eyes are 'glued' to the paper for the next minute or two. When they look up at the subject again their first remark is usually, 'I don't know where I am.' This is because the subject has not been *seen* enough. So always trust in your looking and allow your seeing to direct your pencil marks. As you use your pencil constructively and purposefully allow yourself to become aware even more that every mark you make constructs both tone and direction simultaneously. As a result the illusion of shape and form are represented on the paper. Drawing, by this means, is not really doing the *outline* first and *filling-in* with tone afterwards. Both, as you see them, occur at once. Remember also that as well as looking, you should listen to the sound of the pencil and feel its touch so that you may really enjoy the present action of your drawing.

Stage 7

Now look at the view in your viewfinder and, as before, by comparing all the tones with each other discern those parts which are the next tone. That is, those parts not quite as pale as those for which you have left the white of the paper. Then indicate the outer edges in the same way as before. Because you are now 'tuned in' to your right hemisphere you are probably perceiving tens, if not hundreds, of very subtle gradations of tones. Because of this you may feel unsure about which is the next tone. Please do not be overconcerned about this; just hazard a guess and rely on it. Your guess is an informed one and based upon your honest observation. It will not matter too much at this stage if you have misjudged slightly because your shading will still be quite pale and later on I shall be telling you how you can re-establish any light parts that may have been shaded too dark. Therefore, shade with conviction all the other parts except those which you have honestly discerned and, of course, preserve those lightest parts by keeping them the white of the paper. Remember to allow your looking to help you to see and keep your pencil moving in the various directions that you see the shadows 'moving' across the forms as in Fig. 34e. As you become accustomed to this way of drawing you may soon find it unnecessary, even unhelpful, to indicate the outer edges first, but rather prefer to shade immediately and allow only the edges of your shading to indicate the changes from tone to tone.

Stage 8 (and more)

For all of the remaining stages continue in this way, indicating the outer edges of each next tone first, or not, just as you prefer and find necessary. Figure 34f shows how the third tone has been discerned and left together with the second and first lightest tone. Avoid the strong temptation of wanting to establish and make black those areas that you perceive as the darkest. Be patient and keep your shading evenly and consistently progressive from light to dark. Figure 34g shows that if you do establish and make black those parts which you see as the darkest too soon you are in danger of throwing your entire composition out of balance and making your drawing look like a currant bun or even a fruit cake! Look back now to Exercise 6b and Figs. 22a–f, page 60 and remember how difficult this method was. Therefore, try to understand that if you shade consistently from light to dark, your drawing remains quite pale at the early stages and allows you the relative freedom to alter, correct and amend your drawing. However, if at any stage from when you have established the third or fourth one onwards you need to re-establish a light area (that is, one which you now realize you have made a little too dark) take your eraser and 'draw' these light parts with it. Use then, your eraser as constructively and purposefully as you use your pencil.

Thus allow all parts of your drawing to grow together. Perhaps in a way this approach can be compared to how natural forms grow. For example, all parts of a human baby are young and not fully grown, but the baby is still a complete and perfect form. Not one part of the baby has reached adult proportions. Look now at your drawing. Can you see that though it is 'young' it is also complete at this stage of its development? Many years ago I received a letter from someone whom I have already mentioned earlier in this book and whose advice is still most valuable. Although she was speaking about something quite different I found the following advice also applicable to this approach to drawing. Do you find it so too?

> *No good really leaving one or two areas of ourselves behind and growing in the rest. The neglected ones will at some point come into the foreground and be very noticeable and painful. Then the only thing to do is accept that they are 'younger' than the rest of us and need to 'be brought up to the level of the rest', as someone put it.*
>
> Sister Columba O.S.B.

Look now at the illustrations progressively from start to finish, Fig. 34a–l, and then continue with your drawing in the same way. Bring the softer 4B pencil into play at any time you like until you finish the drawing. You may have discovered already that your thinking in numbers is not only unnecessary but also unhelpful because you just want to detect and see the next tone. Allow this to happen. The system of using numbers is only a preliminary guide to help you to shade progressively from light to dark throughout your drawing as a whole in stages. Indeed using numbers is governed by the left rather than the right hemisphere.

Finally I want to emphasize the point I made at the start of this exercise which is the one embodied in John Ruskin's statement. Rely first and foremost on your looking. Looking helps you to see, and seeing by means of your eyes, your mind and your heart allows your hand to be directed. The drawing on the paper is not so much a representation of the *subject* which you see but rather a representation of your *response* to the subject. Because no one person responds in exactly the same way as another, allow *yourself* to respond as a unique individual, and thus your drawing on the paper will be individually unique. However, more important than this is that you are loving nature. Read Frederick Franck's statement and notice how similar it is, in essence, to that of John Ruskin.

> *It is in order to really see, to see ever deeper, ever more intensely, hence to be fully aware and alive, that I draw what the Chinese call 'The Ten Thousand Things' around me. Drawing is the discipline by which I constantly rediscover the world. I have learned that what I have not drawn, I have not really seen, and that when I start drawing an ordinary thing I realise how extraordinary it is – sheer miracle.*
> Frederick Franck

When you finish, go away from your drawing for a little while and return later on. Then ask yourself the following questions.

'How sensitive am I to the nature and qualities of the pencils? What are they like and what do they like to do?' (Notice that the essence of Exercise 3, the sheet of the senses, is embodied in all of these subsequent exercises.)

'How have I composed the elements of light and shade and the various directions of my marks to form a harmonious drawing which is complete as a whole, and which represents my response, in mind and heart, to that subject?' (Notice that the procedure of assessment and evaluation which you used for your designs in Chapter Two is just the same here.)

Although I said go away from your drawing for a little while and return later on, you probably have realized already that these two questions need to be asked

during the process of drawing as well. Try to remember that you can assess more clearly in a cool and detached manner rather than in the heat of the moment. Otherwise you will not be able to help yourself. Read rule VII (p. 38) again and notice that disobedience to this rule will cloud your being able to assess clearly! If you cannot follow the rule, then go away (even during the process of drawing), engage in a totally different activity for a while and return when you are feeling better and continue to draw. Then assess and evaluate with the same ease and enjoyment as you did when you began.

a

Fig. 35a and b — *Both of these drawings are by Gill Hervey-Murray who attended a 'Drawing for the Terrified' course in 1985. 'I learned a tremendous amount and really enjoyed it. I am sending the very first handkerchief drawing again just to remind you that I didn't have a clue to start with.'*

Now why not try variations of this exercise?

You could screw up a sheet of white paper and place this on another sheet of paper placed flat underneath.

You could set up two arrangements and work them both concurrently. In this way you will be able to put all of the seven main rules into practice so that you will be able to enjoy these games to the maximum.

You could also represent the graduations of tone by means of the three primary colours. Look back to colour plate 5g and that part of Exercise 8 (pp. 71–3) when you produced variations of greys and browns by this means. Look now at your variations of that exercise and choose the three particular hues that enabled you to make the progression of the most 'neutral' tones of grey to black to do this drawing. You should find it great fun to do. Furthermore, it will be very helpful to do before doing the other coloured drawings later on.

b

You have probably realized for some time that I have chosen a subject for this exercise that was as anonymous as possible. Apart from the words 'handkerchief' and perhaps 'folds' and 'creases' there was little to name. This device was to help you to direct your thinking to the right hemisphere. But now look at Fig. 36 and notice how Eirian Short has represented a vast range of tones with multi-directional stitches across the whole of her composition. Can you also see that the variety of planes in the rock formations is not dissimilar to the convolution of folds in a handkerchief? Believe me when I say that if you can perceive tones in any subject in the same way as you did when you drew the handkerchiefs you will be able to draw *any* subject you like.

Fig. 36 — Dawn. Treffgarne Gorge. *Embroidery, Eirian Short, 1986.*

Fig. 37a

Exercise 13 – Fruit and vegetables

First of all become still and quietly attentive by practising the soggy spaghetti arm and golden cord exercises. Spread out some oranges, apples, onions and a few grapes on the table. Allow some to touch each other but also place some apart from each other so that you can see their shadows and reflections on the table. In front of this still-life place your viewfinder. To make it stand up on its own make a 'pair of legs' by clipping two mini bull-dog clips to its lower edge as in Fig. 37a.

Clip a large A3-sized sheet of cartridge paper onto your drawing board and sharpen a 2B and a 4B pencil. Now draw two rectangles onto your sheet of paper that approximate the same proportions as your viewfinder. They need not be the same *size* but they need to be the same *proportion*.

Now follow exactly the same procedure and method of drawing as you did for the handkerchiefs but do two drawings concurrently.

Shift your viewfinder slowly from right to left and then back again from left to right. This enables you to see many different views of the same still-life arrangement. Choose one which you like and keep your viewfinder in that position.

37b

You will notice that if you look with just one eye open you will see a slightly different view from that which you will see with the other eye. Try doing this. Decide now which eye you will use. Pretend that what you see in your viewfinder is a flat two-dimensional image. Make believe that it is a photograph just as it is in Fig. 37b.

Choose one shape near the centre. This may be an apple, an orange or a shadow. Allow your eye to follow the outer contour of this shape and look at it in relation to the vertical and horizontal sides of your viewfinder. Now look to the right and left of this shape and look above and below it. You will see other shapes all of which have outer contours. Look at all these contours in turn and compare one with another and to the sides of your viewfinder. You are now following the same way of estimating and judging positions and proportions as you did when you were drawing the handkerchiefs and allowing your right hemisphere to do the looking for you. Avoid all temptation to name anything at all and to try to work things out logically such as, 'How can I get that apple behind this orange and these shadows in front of those grapes?' If you relax attentively into seeing two-dimensionally instead your resulting drawing will have the appearance of three-dimensional form.

Fig. 38a

Take up your 2B pencil and draw these main contours which you have observed and are still observing within one of your rectangles. As before, these can be broken lines to begin with. Keep your touch on the pencil very gentle so that your marks will appear very pale. Adjust, alter and amend these marks whenever necessary so that you construct the foundation of your drawing with conviction. Your 'scaffolding' should be secure enough for you to remove now the viewfinder altogether. You have now found your view and established this within one of the rectangles on the paper as in Fig. 38a.

Now half close your eyes and compare all the different tones which you see within your still-life arrangement. At this point you will perceive a variety of tones that are caused for two different reasons. First, there are those created by cast light and resulting shadows, just as you saw when you drew the handkerchiefs. Secondly, there are a variety of tones that are intrinsic to the individual objects. For example, your orange may be a mid-tone but lighter than that dark red apple. However, the orange is not as light as those green grapes and the brown wooden table is darkest of all. The degree of darkness or lightness is known as *local colour tone*. Now look again. Look at the parts where the light is cast upon an intrinsically dark object (like the brown table or the dark red apple) and now look

105

38b

at the shadowed areas within an intrinsically light object or group of objects (like the bunch of pale green grapes) and compare the difference. You may be surprised to see what a powerful effect cast light and resulting shadows have. If you had seen *only* the local colour tones you would have been in danger of falling into a trap; because you *knew* these tones, you might have 'fixed' this in your mind and *only* this. As a consequence you would have failed to see the cast light and resulting shadows as strongly as they really are, because you had, in fact, stopped looking. Therefore, *rely on your looking and do this consistently all the time*. From now onwards do not be concerned at all for

the reasons *why* one tone is light and another dark, otherwise your rational left hemisphere will govern your thinking and will probably give you a headache! So, now half close your eyes again, allow them to survey all that you see and identify all those parts that are palest of all (for whatever reasons which you now know you need not worry about). Indicate these on your paper so that you know which parts shall remain white and proceed to shade progressively from light to dark in stages just as you did when you were drawing the handkerchiefs. Look at Fig. 38a–d and realize that the procedure is exactly the same as the preceding exercise. Keep relaxed, attentive and happy all the time. Should

38c

Art is only great if it is in direct contact with cosmic forces and subordinate to them. One senses these laws without realizing it; if one approaches nature not just from the outside, but from within it is necessary not just to look at nature but to live it.

Wassily Kandinsky

My only virtue resides in my submission to instinct. Because I have rediscovered the powers of intuition and allowed them to predominate, I have been able to identify myself with the created world and absorb myself in it.

Claude Monet

38d

you ever catch your left hemisphere chattering away about such names as 'shadows' 'reflections' 'apples' or 'onions' or asking tiresome questions like, 'Is this foreground or is it the background?', and other annoying irrelevances, just put your pencil down and have a rest for a minute or two. Then begin again and allow your right hemisphere to direct your seeing the subject as one harmonious view composed of a variety of shapes, directions and tones, which are all related to each other and form a complete entity.

Fig. 39a

When you have completed one of the early stages so that your drawing is still quite pale, leave it for a while. Move your viewfinder to another position in front of the same still-life arrangement and choose a slightly different view as in Fig. 39. Follow the same drawing procedure as before within your second rectangle. Draw to about the same stage as your first drawing or perhaps slightly further and then leave it for a while. Return to your first drawing for five or ten minutes and then continue with your second drawing for about the same length of time. Alternate between both drawings, working on them concurrently until they are both finished. Refresh your memory about the reasons for this important rule by reading them again on page 35.

When you have completed your drawings, assess and evaluate your work just as you have done before. Furthermore, refer back to your earlier design work and your recent drawings. Spread them all out before you and compare them with each other. What do you notice about your developing sensitivity to the qualities of the materials? What do you notice about your ability to compose lines, edges, contours, shapes and tones in harmony? What moods seem to be evoked through your drawings? (Refer back to p. 47 and remind yourself what Seurat said about how moods can be conveyed by tone.) Are

39b

there any qualities in your earlier work that you did not recognize then but you do now? Keep such scrutiny and questions clear and light always and allow yourself to be pleased with what you do. However, never be satisfied, because satisfaction means literally to have done enough! You realize now that the more you learn, the more there is to learn. This voyage of discovery of yours had only just begun. There are many more delights waiting for you.

> *The man who claims that he knows, knows nothing; but he who claims nothing, knows.*
> From the *Kena-Upanishad*

Now try variations of this way of drawing:

You could change your medium. Try drawing with a ball-point pen, and then a fibre-tipped pen.

Try slightly different methods of using your media. Refer back to Fig. 18 (pp. 52 and 53) and your work for Exercise 5 to help you.

Try using charcoal and then black pastel. These media like to make large marks, so draw on a very large sheet of paper.

You could change to any subject you like, landscapes, seascapes, trees, flowers or figures, so long as you do *not* name it you can do it.

Look at Figs. 40 and 41 to give you some ideas. Now you are ready to play the next game of drawing with colour.

Fig. 40 — Life Drawing. *Pen, ink and wash. Richard Box, 1985.*

Fig. 41 — Hesworth Common. *Pencil drawing. Richard Box, 1985.*

The painter draws with his eyes, not with his hands. Whatever he sees, if he sees it clearly, he can put it down. The putting of it down requires, perhaps, much care and labour but no more muscular agility than it takes to write his name. Seeing clearly is the important thing.

Maurice Grosser

Learning to draw is really a matter of learning to see – to see correctly – and that means a good deal more than looking with the eye.

Kimon Nicolaides

Exercise 14 – Drawing with colour

Before you begin this game, ensure that you have tried all the colour experiments included in Exercise 8 and also my suggestion of drawing the handkerchiefs with just one hue of each of the three primary colours (p. 100). If it has been a long time since you have done these it would be very helpful to draw the handkerchiefs with colour again and also repeat the last two experiments in Exercise 8 (pp. 72 and 73). Look at colour plates 3, 4, 5 and 6 to remind yourself about them. These preliminary exercises will help you to *think* in terms of colour and prepare you for this next game. Furthermore, place the results of these exercises near you so that you can refer to them from time to time.

This game will bring together all the procedures of all the games you have played before into one amazing experience! So that you may enjoy it as much as possible practise now the soggy spaghetti arm and the golden cord exercises and allow yourself to become happily relaxed and contentedly attentive.

Clip a large A3-sized sheet of white cartridge paper to your drawing board and sharpen the six coloured pencils which you used for all the colour experiments in Exercise 8. These are the two different hues of each of the three primary colours: reds, blues and yellows.

Spread out some fruit and vegetables on the table just as you did for the previous exercise such as apples, oranges, a bunch of grapes and a couple of onions. Include a lemon, a few tomatoes and some plums if you like. Choose some objects that are brightly colourful and others, like the onions, that are brown.

Place the viewfinder in front of your still-life arrangement and draw two rectangles on your sheet of paper that approximate to the same proportion as your viewfinder.
Move your viewfinder until you find a section of the entire still-life arrangement which pleases you. Look first at the position and proportion of all the main contours that you see in exactly the same way as you have done before by relating them to each other and to the four sides of the viewfinder. Take up just one of your six coloured pencils and indicate these contours within one of your rectangles with pale broken lines. Now take up another of the coloured pencils

113

Fig. 42 — Woodland scene. *Embroidery, Gill Hervey-Murray, 1986. Embroidered after attending a 'Drawing for the Terrified' course in 1985.*

but choose one hue of one of the two remaining primary colours. With this pencil confirm or amend the position and proportion of these contours but keep your marks very pale. Lastly take up either hue of the third remaining primary colour and with it re-establish the construction of your composition. Adjust, alter and amend whenever necessary. If you wish, return to either of the two colours you began with but remember to keep your marks very pale as in colour plate 8a. So far you have constructed the scaffolding of your drawing in one hue of each of the three primary colours: one red, one blue and one yellow.

Now look at just one part of your still-life arrangement and ask yourself, 'What is its most dominant colour, and with which of my six coloured pencils shall I continue drawing it?' If the part you see is intrinsically a primary colour like yellow (you may have chosen a lemon) then you will, no doubt, choose one of the two hues of yellow that you see as closest to this particular yellow. If the part you see is intrinsically a secondary colour like green (you may have chosen a whole bunch of grapes as one part) then you will choose either that hue of blue or that hue of yellow which is closest to green. Look at this green part again and ask yourself, 'Is this green closer to blue, or is it closer to yellow?' Remember that all answers to such a visual question reside in your looking, so make an informed guess and decide immediately (without dithering!) whether to use the blue or the yellow. If the part you see is a brown or a grey (you may have chosen a shadow on the table) look again and ask yourself, 'Has this brown or grey either a blue, or a red or a yellow aspect?' (Refer to the experiments you did in Exercise 8 and to colour plate 5 and notice how most browns and greys seem to have one colour which is more dominant than any other.) Make a decision instantly and determine what hue of which coloured pencil to use next. Even if the part you see is white, observe whether this white, however slight, has either a pale blue, a pale yellow or a pale red (pink) aspect.

Enjoy looking in this way with ease and contentment. Try not to let your rational and logical left hemisphere predict and work things out for you *beyond* this stage, otherwise you will become troubled. If you are becoming agitated already, take a short rest and read the preceding paragraph again slowly and follow my directions as simply as I have given them.

Now begin drawing that part with the coloured pencil that you have decided is the most appropriate. Colour it all very lightly. Allow your pencil to move in the same way as the inner shapes and forms within this part seem to 'move' in various directions. Now look at another part. Take up another coloured pencil which you believe to be the most appropriate to continue drawing this part with, and draw as before. Proceed to look at every part of your still-life and draw each part with the appropriate colour until all parts are complete at this stage as in colour plate 8b.

Remember that your drawing marks need to be very pale at this early stage. Moreover you do not have to cover the paper with solid colour. Your marks could be hatched lines if you like. In this way quite a lot of the paper will remain white by virtue of the spaces left between your drawing lines. Refer to Fig. 18 (p. 53) and your experiments for Exercise 5 to remind you of the many ways you can use your pencils.

When you have completed this stage, look at your still-life arrangement and at your drawing. Choose a part of your drawing that you wish to continue to develop and decide which is the next hue of what colour you need to use. For example, if this part is a plum and you have already used that blue which is close to purple, you will probably decide to use the red that is close to purple next. Allow this pencil to move in the same way as the inner shapes and forms within this part seem to 'move' *except* on those areas which you see as palest of all. These you preserve as the original first colour. Thus your lightest parts will remain 'coloured whites'. In order to keep the colour and tone consistent throughout your drawing at every stage you will need to draw with this same coloured pencil *all* parts that you believe to contain this colour. To a greater or lesser extent these are all the mid to

Fig. 43a — Landscape drawing.

Fig. 43b — Landscape embroidery.

Lily Westerop made both of these as a result of attending a 'Drawing for the Terrified' course in 1986. Both the drawing and the embroidery were worked in just two hues of each of the three primary colours.

darkly shadowed parts and all those that appear brown and grey. Before you do this refer to your last two experiments for Exercise 8 and colour plates 5 and 6 and notice that all three primary colours are present here also in all the mid to darkly shadowed parts and in all browns and greys. However, they are present in different *quantities* and *proportions*. The greater or lesser amount of any particular colour makes a considerable difference. Now take this same coloured pencil through all those mid to darkly shadowed parts and all those which are brown and grey, but use the appropriate *amount* only, and at this early stage use the colour sparingly as you see in colour plate 8c.

Now select another part of your still-life, decide on which hue of the next colour is necessary, draw this part in the same constructive way as before and leave those areas which you decide are pale enough. Then, as before, take this colour through all parts of your drawing and use only the appropriate amounts that are needed for each individual part as you see in colour plate 8c.

Now look at all the colour plates 8a–d and observe how both tone and colour are constructed simultaneously so that the composition 'grows' and develops as one complete unity at every stage. Choose any hue of any colour in any

order and as many times as you like at any stage. Remember that your continual and consistent looking will direct you to *see* which colour to use at the start of every stage. Your looking will also direct you to see how to move your pencil across the inner shapes, planes, directions and forms of *every* part that comprises the *whole* arrangement. Enjoy every stage as you do it and watch with amazement the miracle of subtle tones and colours of your composition gradually form and develop.

After you have completed one of the early stages of this drawing, leave it for a while and start your second drawing, just as you did in the previous exercise and develop it up to or a little beyond the stage of your first one. Then continue with both drawings concurrently.

Remember to follow the procedure and method of doing these drawings as closely as you can. If you notice parts that you have neglected (for whatever reason) remember that all you have to do is 'to accept that they are "younger" than the rest and need to be "brought up to the level of the rest." ' If you do this you will soon realize that not only will everything be well, but everything *is* well.

Remember to follow also the seven rules (from p. 34 onwards) that govern all the games in this book so that you may enjoy playing them to the full.

Fig. 44 — *Two pieces by Joan Hoare after attending a 'Drawing for the Terrified' course in 1986.*

44a Christmas Rose. *Watercolour, 1986.*

44b Christmas Rose. *Embroidery, 1986.*

> *Not only* will *everything be all right; but*
> *everything* is *all right.*
>   Hubert Box

When you finish, ask yourself those questions which help you to assess and evaluate what you have done and what you do. Remember to keep your questions cool in mind, but warm in heart, so that although you may never be satisfied you will always be pleased with the way you played these games and with your consequent results on paper.

Now you are ready to try numerous variations of this game of drawing with colour. For the time being remain with the same medium of coloured pencils. (It is beyond the scope of this book for me to explain how you can use soft chalk pastels, oil pastels, watercolour, gouache and even oil or acrylic paints. Nevertheless, if you feel inspired to have a go, then do so gladly!)

Try the same subject of a still-life group of fruit and vegetables but now include more hues of the primary colours at the early stages and bring secondary coloured pencils at the later stages of your drawing. In this way you will achieve a more exact representation of local colours and a richer density of tones.

Try as many different subjects and scenes as you like. Buildings, street scenes, gardens, parks, herbaceous borders, river banks, ponds, greenhouses, conservatories, industrial estates, docklands, wharfs and estuaries are all available for you, so long as you want to have a go.

Fig. 45 — Vase of Flowers. *Embroidery, Sally Burwell, 1986. Embroidered after attending a 'Drawing for the Terrified' course in 1985.*

'It has been an inspiration to me to start drawing and looking at things in an entirely new light.'

Fig. 46 — Snow Scene. *Embroidery, Richard Box, 1982.*

At this point you are ready for the next game which is to translate one of your coloured drawings into fabric collage and machine and hand embroidery.

Fig. 47a *Still life, drawing (1986);*

Jennie Parry who made these has used just two hues of each of the three primary colours for both the drawing and the embroidery.

47b *Still life, embroidery (1986).*

Chapter Four

FABRIC COLLAGE AND EMBROIDERY

How you interpret your designs and translate your drawings into embroidery is now entirely up to you. The embroideries that are illustrated in this book show many different approaches and techniques and are here to help you. Some come from the past and others are of today; some traditional, others more experimental. Some have been made by professionals; others by amateurs. All have been done with care and attention. Indeed some have been made by students who have attended either one of my courses, 'Designing for the Nervous and Anxious' or 'Drawing for the Terrified and Afraid'. Some have attended both. Afterwards they have taken their work home and employed whatever approach and technique they wanted. Try to be encouraged and inspired rather than daunted by the examples. All the embroiderers were beginners once!

In this chapter I shall not be concerning myself with showing you lots of different methods. I want to show you just one approach. Just as my approach to preparing yourself by relaxing attentively, my procedure for designing and my method of drawing are each just one way – and not the only way – so also will I now show you just one way of translating one of your coloured drawings into embroidery. This is our last game.

Exercise 15 – Design and drawing with fabric and thread

I have been evolving this approach to develop my embroideries for the past ten years. Because it has been a source of great joy and pleasure to me, I would like to share it with you now. In some respects it is quite precise; therefore, you will need to follow the directions carefully. However, in other respects it is very free and flexible. You will discover that within its main framework you can include many variations of your own invention. This approach has three main stages. Although it is possible to overlap them (and I have discovered that I find it necessary to overlap the last two stages) they are set out here as three individual stages so that the whole approach is as clear as possible for you to follow. Before you begin, remember to practise the soggy spaghetti arm and the golden cord exercises often and at any time as you like. Also remember the seven main guiding rules. All seven are as equally applicable to this game as to all the others. Although I shall not remind you of them during the course of this chapter, please try not to forget them, not even the one concerning concurrent work. I try to have several embroideries on the go at one time, so that I can transfer new discoveries quickly from one to another and also to solve certain problems with comparative ease.

Fig. 48

Stage 1

You need to choose first one of your coloured drawings. Lay them all out before you and select one because the balance and harmony of its composition pleases you. I have chosen one of my drawings of my 'Poppies and Daisies' series. See colour plates 10a–d and Fig. 48.

Then take a sheet of tracing paper that is the same size as your drawing and trace the main contours and shapes of your composition. You could colour the various parts to distinguish one from another more clearly if you wish.

If you want your embroidery to be the same size as your drawing this tracing will act as your paper pattern. If you want your embroidery to be larger than your drawing, you will need to find a large sheet of paper which is in the same proportion as your drawing.

If you want your embroidery to be very large you may have to join several sheets of paper together with sticky tape. This is what you do to enlarge your drawing. First, fold both the tracing paper and the large sheet of paper into 16 equal rectangles, by first folding each in half, then in quarters, then in eighths and lastly into sixteenths. Secondly, unfold both sheets of paper and rule three horizontal and three vertical lines where you see the resulting creases on the paper. Then look at the top left rectangle on the tracing paper where you will see some of your drawing lines. Judge the position and direction of these lines in relation to the four sides of this rectangle just as you did when you were looking through the viewfinder. Then draw a close approximation of these lines in the same position and angled at the same directions within the top left rectangle of your large sheet of paper. Now look again at your drawing on the tracing paper and particularly at the three

rectangles closest to the one at the top left. Look at the one to its immediate right, the one below it and that one that lies diagonally below and right of it. Notice the position and directions of your lines there, and then reproduce a close approximation of these lines within the corresponding rectangles on your large sheet of paper. Continue in this way until you complete your enlarged drawing. You could colour the various parts, as before, so that you may more easily distinguish one part from another if you wish. This now becomes your paper pattern.

You now need to find a firm length of fabric, such as hessian, the size of which should be about 10–15cm (4–6in.) larger than your paper pattern. This is to be the backing fabric of your embroidery and needs this margin all round the edge so that you have enough material to turn the edges when you stretch it after you have finished. Choose a colour that is one of the most dominant in your original drawing. You will discover that it is not necessary to cover the backing fabric completely when you apply other fabrics and threads. You may decide to leave some of it peeping through as an integral part of your design.

Put the paper pattern onto your backing fabric and place them on your work table somewhere near the centre close to you. Also put your original coloured drawing in a position so that you can see it clearly as in Fig. 49.

Now look at your original drawing in terms of the coloured parts in particular. You know that reds, blues and yellows are present because you used those coloured pencils to draw it with. You probably see greens, oranges and purples, and perhaps there are some browns, greys and 'coloured whites'. These are the colours of fabric that you will need to select. Look at your coloured drawing again and see which colours are most apparent in quantity and those which

Fig. 49

appear least. This will direct you to select the amount of each colour of fabric scraps you will need. Now rummage through your rag bag and select quite small pieces of any kind and sort of fabric scraps you have, so long as they are not too thick. You could include patterned and multi-coloured fabrics if you like. Now sort these out into piles of individual colours. Include lots of different hues of that colour for each pile. Then take a pair of sharp scissors and start to cut these scraps into tiny pieces. Some can be as small as your little finger nail, others a little larger. Cut some with straight edges and some with curved edges. Some could be long and thin, others short and more square. Thus vary

the kind of size and shape of each tiny piece. When you finish cutting, place each small pile of every hue within its own colour category and it would help you to place each colour next to its own as in the spectrum. When you finish cutting altogether you should have a semi-circle, rather like a rainbow, arranged on the table around your hessian backing fabric.

If you have found it necessary to include browns, greys and whites include these somewhere in your rainbow arrangement. My arrangement in Fig. 49 consists mainly of reds and greens in terms of amount, then blues, yellows and whites and lastly, oranges and purples. There are no browns or greys.

Put some P.V.A. glue into a small jar and find a small brush. Put them to one side for a moment. Choose the colour you wish to start with and cut out all those parts which relate to this colour from your paper pattern. Throw them away and leave the remainder of the pattern on the hessian backing fabric. You will use the pattern rather like you use a stencil. Now look at your original drawing carefully. Choose one of these parts and notice the variety of hues and tones of that one colour within this part. Now take up your brush and dip it into the glue, allowing only a little to adhere to the bristles. Then take the brush to one of the tiny pieces of material which approximates one of these colour hues; lift it up, turn it upside-down and stick it in the appropriate spot on the hessian backing fabric. Continue in this manner until that part is completely composed with the variety of tones and hues of that colour that equate with those in the original drawing. Proceed to do the same for all those parts that are composed of this colour as in Fig. 49.

Then choose the next colour that you want to continue with. Cut all parts that relate to this colour out from your paper pattern and proceed as you did before. Continue in this way until all parts of your fabric collage are composed with the variety of tones and hues which approximate those in your original coloured drawing. As you do this it is important to be guided by the rhythm and pattern of the pencil marks in your original drawing because these have helped to contribute to its total harmony. Emulate this kind of rhythm and pattern in the way you lay the direction of your small pieces. Exaggerate this if you wish. Conversely, if you feel that this needs less emphasis, understate it. Indeed, if you feel that you need to, exaggerate or understate the range of textures, tones

and even the intensity of colour. Allow yourself to express your original experience as powerfully or as gently as you wish. Remember that your original drawing does not so much represent what you saw but rather it expresses your *response* to what you saw and, indeed, experienced by means of your other senses as well. Thus, visual accuracy is not necessarily the only quality that you may be seeking, if at all. 'Art is a lie that makes us realize the truth' said Picasso. Matisse also said 'Exactitude is not the truth'. Now be reassured by Matisse about how you can express your feelings by the arrangement of the many elements in your composition. Also refer back to Seurat's statement (p. 47) about such elements of colour, tone and line.

> *What I am after, above all, is expression. Expression, to my way of thinking, does not consist of the passion mirrored upon a human face or betrayed by a violent gesture. The whole arrangement of my picture is expressive. The place occupied by figures or objects, the empty space around them, the proportions, everything plays a part.*
> Henri Matisse
>
> *Composition is the art of arranging in a decorative manner the various elements at the painter's disposal for the expression of his feelings. In a picture every part will be visible and will play the role conferred upon it, be it principle or secondary. All that is not useful in the picture is detrimental. A work of art must be harmonious in its entirety; for superfluous details would in the mind of the beholder encroach upon the essential elements.*
> **Henri Matisse**

When you are at that stage when the paper pattern has completed its function, you are now able to see your composition of fabric pieces as a whole. Engage in the practice of assessing and evaluating your work at this stage in the same way as you have done before. In order that your composition expresses your feelings as clearly and as effectively as possible, compose your harmony by balancing similar and complementary elements together. For example, if one particular colour seems too dominant, balance this by including a little of the complementary colour. If you have laid the fabric pieces all in one direction, lay some in the other direction. If all your pieces are too much the same size, include some larger and some smaller pieces. If the fabric pieces you have used seem too much the same texture, try balancing matt with shiny pieces and try laying transparent pieces such as nets and laces over the opaque ones. Look at Fig. 50. Although the composition is somewhat crude at this stage, it is, however, complete in its structural foundations. It is the next stage which will bring refinements.

> *We never look at just one thing; we are always looking at the relation between things and ourselves.*
>
> **John Berger**

Stage 2

Bring out your sewing machine. It needs to be able to do a zig-zag stitch, to be able to drop its feed and to have a darning foot attachment. Set the machine at its widest zig-zag stitch, drop the feed and attach the darning foot. Select two or three different hues of your machine embroidery threads of each of the colours which are present in the fabric scraps you used for your collage. Choose a variety of different kinds of threads. Some can be matt and others shiny. By having a varied choice you will be able to continue balancing complementary and similar elements as before.

Choose a colour and its particular hue that you want to start with. Thread your sewing machine with it and wind several bobbins with any colour. Set the tension of your machine according to the instructions in your handbook so that it sews freely and easily over the material with the darning foot attachment and the feed dropped. Practise on a spare piece of hessian until this is achieved.

Now sew across all those pieces of fabric which match the colour, tone and hue of the thread. Sometimes sew on one side of the fabric pieces. At this early stage sew very sparingly. When you finish, change the colour, tone or hue of the thread and sew sparingly across or on one side of those pieces of fabric that match this second thread. (You may not need to change the thread on your bobbin.) Continue in this way until all the tiny pieces of fabric are tacked onto the hessian with their appropriately matching colours. As you do this, be aware that you are not only applying the pieces of fabric to the hessian with the thread but you are also drawing with it too. Your choice of colour, tone and hue, and the way you direct your sewing stitches are as much part of the construction of your composition as everything you have done before in all the exercises for designing and drawing. So be guided, as always, by looking, touching and even listening to what you are doing and refer to your original drawing from time to time.

When you have tacked all the pieces, compare your embroidery with your original drawing. Stand away from them. Assess and evaluate in the way that you

are now accustomed and decide which colour, tone and hue of thread needs to be used to develop the construction of your embroidery. Be aware also of the kind of texture of the thread you use next. Once you have decided, thread your sewing machine with the next thread and continue sewing with the same kind of relaxed attention as before. You could alter the width of your stitch from the widest zig-zag to the straight running stitch. Vary or limit this according to the needs of your composition whenever you want. To a greater or lesser extent you can now take this coloured thread across other colours in the following way. If the thread you are using now is red, you could take it sparingly across all hues of red and also across its adjacent colours within the spectrum – namely, oranges and purples, because red is a component of these two colours. You could also take this red thread across those areas of green that need either 'softening' or darkening. Refer to colour plate 6 and notice how a similar effect has been achieved by such means. Furthermore, you could take this thread across all other coloured fabrics in varying quantities and proportions so long as they are the same tonal value as the thread. For example, if this red thread is a very pale red (a pink) you could take it across all pale yellows, blues and greens. You can now employ this approach with all the threads at your disposal. In this way you will achieve an integration of your composition and the beginnings of that refinement which I spoke of earlier.

Stage 3

After you have taken a number of machine embroidery threads through your composition, and it is complete at that stage, you could start to do some hand stitching. After you have taken a number of threads through your composition by hand, and it is once again complete at that stage, you could then return to your sewing machine and lock or couch some of your hand embroidery. I mentioned earlier that these last two stages could overlap each other. It all depends on you and your decision concerning the balance and harmony of your composition. Look at Fig. 51 to see my completed embroidery. Your choice of threads for hand stitching can be as varied or as limited as you like. Why not try using knitting and weaving yarns as well as traditional embroidery threads? Vary or limit the type of stitches you use in a similar way. This approach does not necessarily require a vast knowledge of stitch techniques. I shall always remember what the well-known embroiderer and inspiring teacher Constance Howard said the very first time I met her – 'It doesn't matter if you don't know any stitches, just make them up as you go along.' One of the most important things to remember is that your embroidery expresses you in a harmonious way – so try to remember to *enjoy* doing it.

> *To create a work of art is to create a world.*
> **Wassily Kandinsky**

When you have completed this embroidery, or your concurrent series of embroideries, try as many variations of this approach as you like. Try other subjects and themes. Try many varied

Fig. 50

Fig. 51

sizes of embroideries. Adapt and develop this approach in as many ways as occur to you.

In the same way adapt and develop your approaches to designing and systems of drawing as well. You are now ready to move away from those in this book. By all means keep using any of those procedures which you still find useful, but do not allow them to constrict you. Allow yourself to evolve your own individual and ever-changing methods which express you as a unique and an exceptionally creative person, which indeed you are.

POSTSCRIPT

Design, drawing and embroidery as devotion

If you have read thus far and practised all of the games in this book you will have realized that you have only just begun your wonderful journey of 'serious fun'. The world is now your oyster, and you may continue to devote yourself to playing as many games as you like. You now know that such games can be more than frivolous pastimes but activities of great import, of devotion, even of prayer. However, they should not be heavy, laborious or sanctimonious; rather, they should be light, easy and joyful. At the start of the book I told you a story. Now the book is almost finished I want to conclude it by telling you another one. Just as the first story intends to alleviate our worries, anxieties and fears, so also does this one tell of how futile and unnecessary it is to worry about past events and to be anxious about future predictions; because, if we do, we are in danger of missing all the delights that we may enjoy now in the present. The final line of the story is so concise and succinct that its meaning is not immediately clear. Often it has been misinterpreted as being hedonistic but you who have practised the games in this book know better. Ever since I first heard this story I have told it to all the students who attend any one of my courses. In repeated telling it has become somewhat 'embroidered'. Indeed only a year ago one of my students discovered the original version which even I had not read. It is an ancient parable which you may like to seek out one day. In the meantime I shall tell you my elaborated version.

The Strawberry

Once upon a time there lived a lady who had won many golden medals in the Olympic Games for her fast running. Indeed, she was the fastest runner in the whole wide world! One day she found herself in a jungle being chased by a tiger. Very soon she realized that her ability to run fast was not much help to her now, because the tiger was faster than she. Moreover this tiger was extremely hungry. Suddenly she arrived at a precipice, steep, sheer and seemingly abysmal. In about a millionth of a second she had to decide whether to be gobbled up by the tiger or to chance to luck and jump to wherever . . . ? and to whatever . . . ? She jumped.

As she descended she very soon saw what was awaiting her at the bottom of this now-not-so-apparently abysmal drop . . . two thousand and three crocodiles with large jaws agape, as if saying, 'Yum, yum, here comes something nice to eat.'

As the lady was falling at an ever increasing rate, she noticed a branch protruding from the side of the precipice a little further down. She managed to catch it with her hands just in time. 'Phew!' she thought to herself as she

Fig. 52 — A plate of strawberries. *Embroidery, Heide Jenkins, 1982. (Collection of the Embroiderers' Guild)*

dangled there. Then she heard a gnawing sound. When she looked at the root of this branch she saw two mice, one was white and the other was black, and they were both chewing the root voraciously. Fortunately, she saw also a strawberry nearby, growing from the side of the precipice. She reached out one hand, picked it and she had only to take one bite to discover that it tasted absolutely wonderful.

Do not be anxious about tomorrow; tomorrow will look after itself.

Matthew 6.34

BIBLIOGRAPHY

Arnason, H.H. *A history of modern art.* Thames and Hudson. Revised edition, 1977.

Bloomer, Carolyn M. *Principles of visual perception.* Van Nostrand Reinhold Company, 1976.

Edwards, Betty. *Drawing on the right side of the brain.* Souvenir Press, 1981.

Franck, Frederick. *The zen of seeing.* Vintage Books (originally published by Alfred A. Knopf), 1973.

Hamilton, George Heard. *Painting and sculpture in Europe 1880–1940.* Penguin Books Limited. Revised edition; reprinted 1978.

Lowenfeld, V. *Creative and mental growth.* The Macmillan Company. Fifth edition, 1970.

Malins, Frederick. *Understanding paintings – the elements of composition.* Phaidon Press Limited, 1980.

McKim, Robert H. *Experiences in visual thinking.* Wadsworth Incorporated. Second edition, 1980.

Murray, Peter and Linda. *A dictionary of art and artists.* Penguin Books Limited. Third edition; reprinted 1975.

Mussen, Paul H., Conger, John J. and Kagan, Jerome. *Child development and personality.* Harper and Row. Fifth edition, 1979.

Richter, Irma A. *The notebooks of Leonardo da Vinci.* Oxford University Press, 1980.

Shree Purohit Swami, and Yeats, W.B. (trans.) *The ten principal Upanishads.* Faber and Faber Limited, 1970.

Swami Vivekananda. *Work and its secret.* J.N. Dey at Union Press. Seventh impression, 1976.

GLOSSARY

I include this section because I know how tiresome it is to try to find that page in a book where the definition of a particular term, word or phrase has been explained but is now forgotten. Words and phrases can have different meanings for different people at different times and in different places. My definitions may not meet the approval or agreement of all. However, the following descriptions refer to how I have intended these terms to be understood in the text of this book.

Analytical   Refers to the ability to abstract particular parts or specific relations from generalities.

Attention   The ability to be fully observant without being distracted by irrelevances.

Assessment   The ability to observe and understand that which has been done and is being done.

Colour   The constituent parts of decomposed rays of light and the general name given to pigments such as red, orange, yellow, green, blue and purple.

Complementary   Refers to an element or quality which usually contrasts with or is in opposition to another element or quality.

Composition   The harmonious relation of all parts of a whole such as a design, drawing or embroidery.

Cross hatching   A method of shading by means of crossed parallel lines.

Designing   The process of planning and organizing all the parts to compose a harmonious whole.

Drawing   The representation and realization of a person's response to the world.

Elements (or formal elements)   Those components that exist in physical substances such as edge, shape, form, tone, colour and texture.

Evaluation   The ability to recognize the value in that which has been done and is being done for present and future use.

Form   A shape understood in three dimensions.

Form (to)   To construct and make.

Harmony   The balanced combination of various qualities and elements usually comprising those that are both similar and complementary.

Hatching   A method of shading with parallel lines.

Holistic   Refers to the ability to understand whole things altogether at once.

Hue   The quality that distinguishes one particular kind of colour from another such as a scarlet red from a crimson red.

Intuitive   Refers to the ability to make leaps of insight without analytical, logical and rational reasoning.

Knowledge   That which is discovered and understood (an empirical definition only).

Line   A term used in three different ways: (a) that which represents an edge or contour of a shape; (b) a very thin shape; (c) that which denotes direction.

Logical   Refers to the ability to reason and to reach conclusions by following an ordered sequence of thought.

Local colour   The intrinsic colour of any particular object such as a *red* apple.

Local colour tone   The intrinsic tonal value of any particular object such as a *dark* red apple or a *pale* green grape.

Perception   The detection and recognition of sensations and stimuli within the environment.

Process   The activity of doing and proceeding with awareness.

Rational   Refers to the ability to make decisions based upon information, facts and reasons.

Realization   That which has been made manifest and real such as a design, drawing or embroidery.

Recipe   A particular way or procedure of engaging in an activity by means of certain rules.

Rules   Guidelines to assist the process or procedure of any given activity, exercise or game.

Sensitivity   The ability to be exceptionally aware and appreciative of impressions.

Shade   A dark tone.

Shade (to)   To darken, such as with pencil lines in drawing.

Shape   An area perceived in two dimensions.

Spacial   Refers to the ability to understand how individual parts relate to one another.

Texture   The surface quality of any physical substance.

Tint   A light or pale tone.

Tone (or tonal value)   The quality that distinguishes anything within the range between light and dark.

INDEX OF NAMES

INDEX